The Family Historian's Pocket Dictionary

compiled by

STUART A. RAYMOND

Published by
The Federation of Family History Societies
(Publications) Ltd.,
Units 15-16, Chesham Industrial Estate,
Oram Street, Bury,
Lancashire, BL9 6EN, U.K.

in association with
S.A. & M.J. Raymond
P.O. Box 35, Exeter EX1 3YZ
Email: samjraymond@btopenworld.com
Http: www.samjraymond.btinternet.co.uk/igb.htm

ISBNs:
Federation of Family History Societies: 1-86006-172-9
S.A. & M.J. Raymond: 1-899668-32-2

First published 2003

Printed and bound by the Alden Group, Oxford OX2 0EF

Introduction

The study of family history is now one of the most popular hobbies in the western world, not just in England and Wales, but also in all those countries where British migrants have settled in the last few centuries - North America, Australia, New Zealand, South Africa, *etc.* The range of resources for family historians is increasing rapidly, and continually needs fresh description and explanation. It is noteworthy, for example, that the internet, which now has an important place in genealogical research, is barely mentioned in the books listed at the end of this introduction.

The purpose of this book is to act as a ready reference source in which all genealogists researching in England and Wales will be able to find definitions of terms, and pointers to the information they seek. The emphasis here has been on the importance of books and, to a lesser extent, the internet, in genealogical research. Archives are obviously important, but too often they are consulted first, whereas they should be consulted last. Books (and I use the term here to encompass CD's and microfiche as well) should always be consulted before you visit the archives: they will help you find your way around your record office, and greatly increase your efficiency in using archives. The information you need may already be in print, or on the internet; if so, it will be much easier to find than if you have to search the archives. I hope that users will pay particular attention to the entries for 'bibliographies', 'libraries', and 'books', since these are the primary ways into the information that is being sought. I make no apology for repeatedly emphasising this point throughout this book.

In this dictionary, I have tried to indicate the basic books available on each subject. These books are usually referred to in the text by authors' names; full citations are given at the end of each entry. I have also tried to identify good examples of source material in print. Many record societies and other publishers have published numerous parish registers, wills, estate records, and other genealogical sources. It is a good idea to examine these publications before visiting archives, so that you can see the type of information particular sources are likely to yield. Such books cited here are mentioned as examples only; many other titles could have been listed, and you should try to identify similar titles for the area(s) where you think your ancestors lived.

I have also listed some of the more useful websites. However, this book cannot possibly be a substitute for my *F.F.H.S. web directories* and *British genealogical library guides*. It is intended to signpost sources of information, not to be a comprehensive treatise or directory.

This volume is a dictionary, and hence is arranged alphabetically by subject. The alphabetical arrangement does, however, ignore relationships between subjects. Consequently, within each entry I have tried to direct readers to related topics by asterisking those terms which have separate entries.

Some subjects I have deliberately not covered. There are no entries here for particular counties (although off-shore crown dependencies, i.e. the Channel Isles and the Isle of Man, are covered), nor for specific occupations; adequate treatment of these subjects would have doubled the length of this book. I have only covered other countries to the extent that is relevant in tracing English migrants. Subjects treated have been selected for their relevance to genealogical research, rather than their general historical interest - hence there are no entries for topics such as 'inflation' or 'pinfold', 'reeve' or 'headland'. Each entry is intended as a very brief and succinct introduction to its subject, bearing in mind that many subjects in themselves require - and, in many cases, have already received - book-length treatment.

This book relies heavily on the works of hundreds of other authors. I am particularly indebted to the authors of previous genealogical dictionaries, which include:

- FITZHUGH, TERRICK V.H. *The dictionary of genealogy,* 5th ed., revised by Susan Lumas. A & C. Black, 1998.
- HEY, DAVID. *The Oxford companion to local and family history.* Oxford University Press, 1996.
- HEY, DAVID. *The Oxford dictionary of local and family history.* Oxford University Press, 1997.
- SAUL, PAULINE. *The family historians enquire within.* 5th ed. F.F.H.S., 1995.

Fitzhugh is the most useful of these for the genealogist, although Hey's *Companion* includes much more historical background.

There are two other books which I have had constantly at my side whilst writing this one:

- HERBER, MARK D. *Ancestral trails: the complete guide to British genealogy and family history.* Sutton Publishing / Society of Genealogists, 1997.
- BEVAN, AMANDA. *Tracing your ancestors in the Public Record Office.* 6th ed. Public Record Office, 2002.

Herber's guide is an authoritative and comprehensive textbook; Bevan has written an extensive guide to the genealogical resources of the major British archive repository, whose holdings are repeatedly referred to here.

I have also, of course, consulted many hundred books on specific topics. In order to identify them, the volumes of my own *British genealogical library guides* have been essential.

I am grateful to Cynthia Hanson, who has typed this book, to Bob Boyd, who has seen it through the press, and to the officers of the Federation of Family History Societies, who continue to support my genealogical writings. I am grateful too to my wife and family, who have long been used to papers and books scattered across the lounge-room floor.

Stuart A. Raymond

A

A2A

Access to Archives is a major web-based database
established by the *Historical Manuscripts Commission. It
provides online access to the archives catalogues of
innumerable English record offices, and should be checked
by all genealogists.

Web Page:
- A2A: Access to Archives
  www.a2a.pro.gov.uk

Abbreviations

Abbreviations and acronyms are frequently encountered in
genealogy. Some of the most common are listed here. For the
abbreviations of county names, see *Chapman county codes.

A.G.R.A.	Association of Genealogists and Researchers in Archives
A2A	Access to Archives
Admon.	Letters of administration
Ag. Lab	Agricultural labourer
B.A.L.H.	British Association for Local History
B.Ts	Bishops' transcripts
Big R	*British Isles Genealogical Register*
B.R.A.	British Records Association
Bt.	Baronet
C.R.O.	County record office
Cal.	Calendar
C.A.M.P.O.P.	Cambridge Group for the History of Population and Social Structure
Co.	County
D.N.B.	*Dictionary of National Biography*
Esq.	Esquire
f.	folio

F.F.H.S.	Federation of Family History Societies
F.H.G.	Fellow of the Institute of Heraldic and Genealogical Studies
F.H.N.D.	*Family history news and digest*
F.H.S.	Family history society
F.R.C.	Family Records Centre
F.S.	Female servant
F.S.G.	Fellow of the Society of Genealogists
F.W.K.	Framework knitter
fo.	folio
G.R.O.	General Register Office
Gent.	Gentleman
Goons	Guild of One Name Studies
H.M.C.	Historical Manuscripts Commission
I.G.I.	*International Genealogical Index*
I.H.G.S.	Institute of Heraldic and Genealogical Studies
I.P.M.	Inquisition Post Mortem
J.P.	Justice of the Peace
Knt	Knight
L.D.S.	Latter Day Saints
lic.	[married by] licence
M.I.	Monumental inscription
M.S.	Male servant
mem.	membrane
Mss.	Manuscript
N.I.P.R.	*National Index of Parish Registers*
N.R.A.	National Register of Archives
N.L.W.	National Library of Wales
O.N.S.	Office for National Statistics
o.t.p.	Of this parish
ob	obit (died)
O.P.A.C.	On-line Public Access Catalogue
P.C.C.	Prerogative Court of Canterbury
P.C.Y.	Prerogative Court of York
P.R.O.	Public Record Office
Pec.	Peculiar
PROCAT	Public Record Office on-line catalogue
R.D.	Registration District

S.O.G.   Society of Genealogists
Ts   Typescript
V.C.H.   *Victoria County History*

Accounts

Thousands of accounts, from a wide variety of sources, survive in record offices. Most of them identify people - accountants, creditors, debtors, servants, tradesmen, ratepayers, *etc., etc.*

Accounts have been prepared for *churchwardens, *overseers (see *poor law), *households, *manors, (see *estate records), ecclesiastical bodies, and many other institutions. It is well worth trying to identify any accounts relating to the areas your ancestors came from, in case they may be mentioned.

Achievements

Armorial bearings shown in full, and including *coats of arms, crest, helm, *etc.*

Act Books

Act books record the proceedings of ecclesiastical courts. They were usually written in very crabbed Latin before 1733, and therefore are difficult to use; nevertheless, since the work of ecclesiastical courts was wide-ranging in scope, it is quite possible to find ancestors mentioned in them.

Further Reading:

- BRINKWORTH, E.R.C., ed. *The Archdeacon's court: liber actorum 1584.* 2 vols. Oxfordshire Record Society **23-4**. 1942-6.

Administration Bonds

When a person died without leaving a will, the next of kin, or perhaps a friend, would take out letters of administration, and would be required to enter into a bond to "well and truely administer" the deceased's estate "according to the law". Administration bonds are usually filed with probate inventories. Before 1733, a portion of the bond is in Latin; however, the wording is usually in a set form, and, indeed, many can be found on printed forms. Administration bonds provide the names and parishes of the administrator and the deceased, the name of the official who granted administration, witnesses, and a date by which the inventory had to be exhibited in court. They are to be found with other *probate records.

Adoption

Prior to 1927, no formal records of adoption exist, other than the occasional deed entered into by parents and adopter. The Adopted Childrens Register began in that year, and indexes can be consulted at the *Family Records Centre. The Adoption Act 1976 gives adoptees the right to information on their birth, and access to their adoption file; details are available on the web at the National Statistics site:

Web Pages:
- Adoption
  www.familyrecords.gov.uk/adoptionmain.htm

- National Statistics: Adoptions
  www.statistics.gov.uk/nsbase/registration/Adoptions.asp

- Tracing the Birth Parents of Adopted Persons in England and Wales
  www.ffhs.org.uk/General/Help/Adopted.htm

Further reading:
- STAFFORD, G. *Where to find adoption records: a guide for counsellors.* 2nd ed. British Agencies for Adoption and Counselling, 1993.

Advowson

The right of presentation to an ecclesiastical living, owned by a patron who presents the priest to the bishop for institution and induction.

Age of Consent and Majority

Prior to 1969, the age at which a person was legally considered to be an adult was 21. This was important for purposes of inheritance; for the landed classes it marked the end of wardship. The age of consent was variable until 1929, when it was fixed at 16. Child marriage was common amongst the middle and upper classes in the medieval period, although it was frowned on by the church.

Further Reading:

- FURNIVALL, FREDERICK J., ed. *Child-marriages, divorces and ratifications &c., in the Diocese of Chester, A.D. 1561-6.* Early English Text Society. Original series **108**. 1897.

Alias

An alias is an alternative *surname, used interchangeably. Aliases are quite common, and genealogists need to be aware that a new alias could replace an old surname. Surnames are often regarded as unchanging, but the widespread use of aliases disproves this assumption.

Aliens

See Immigrants and Aliens

Alumni

See University Registers

Ancestors

Your ancestors include everyone who has contributed to the genes you carry, i.e. all lines of descent, both male and female. This contrasts with your family, which is traced in the male line only.

Ancestral File

This is an on-line collection of pedigrees which has been compiled by members of the *Church of Jesus Christ of Latter Day Saints and other genealogists. It is international in scope, but with a heavy American bias.

11

Web Page:
• Ancestral File: Searching
  www.lds-family-history.org/rookie/afsearch.htm

Annuities/Annuitants and Tontines

An annuity is an annual amount payable for a fixed term of years, or for life. A tontine is an annuity which is shared by subscribers to a loan, and which increases in value as subscribers die, the last surviving subscriber(s) receiving the whole of the interest. The records of 17-18th century government annuities and tontines are at the *Public Record Office in classes NDO1-3; they give names, addresses, ages at entry, and the dates of first payments, together with some marriage and death dates, and wills.

Further Reading:
• LEESON, F. L. *A Guide to the records of British state tontines and life annuities of the seventeenth and eighteenth centuries.* Society of Genealogists, 1968.

Apprentices

Apprenticeship is still with us to a limited extent, but in previous centuries it was much more important than it is today. Indeed, the Statute of Apprentices, 1563, forbade anyone to practice a trade without having served a seven year apprenticeship. With amendments, this remained law until 1814.

The records relating to apprenticeship are of great value to genealogists. A boy entering apprenticeship (a few girls did so too) was bound to his master by an apprenticeship indenture; his parents (or, in the case of paupers, the overseers) had to pay a premium to bind the boy. Few indentures survive, except amongst the records of the overseers of the poor; however, many apprenticeship registers are available. The Corporation of London and the city livery companies have particularly rich collections, currently being indexed by Cliff Webb in his *London livery companies apprenticeship registers* series published by the Society of Genealogists. Many other corporate boroughs and guilds also have registers. Apprenticeship records may also be found amongst business records, and with the archives of charities.

In addition, the *Public Record Office holds a series of apprenticeship books (IR1) running from 1710 to 1811, arising from the operation of an Act of Parliament which made stamp duty payable on apprenticeship indentures. These books record the names, trades and addresses of the masters, the names of apprentices, and the dates of indentures. Indexes of masters' names 1710-62, and of apprentices names 1710-74, are available at the *Public Record Office (IR17) and the Society of Genealogists; these have been published on 138 fiche as *Unpublished finding aids for genealogical research, series two: the Society of Genealogists apprenticeship index.* Harvester Press Microform, 1985, which may be available in major research libraries. These indexes are about to be made available on the internet at **www.englishorigins.com**

Web Sites:
- Apprenticeship Records in Guildhall Library
  **www.cityoflondon.gov.uk/leisure_heritage/libraries_
  archives_museums_galleries/assets/pdf/pb_
  apprentices.pdf**

- Apprenticeship Records as Sources for Genealogy
  catalogue.pro.gov.uk/Leaflets/ri2187.htm

Further Reading:
- THOMPSON, KATHRYN M. 'Apprenticeship and bastardy records', in THOMPSON, K.M., ed. *Short guides to records. Second series, guides 25-48.* Historical Association, 1997, 29-32.

- WILLIS, ARTHUR J. *A calendar of Southampton apprenticeship registers, 1609-1740,* ed. A. L. Merson. Southampton Records series **12**. 1968.

- BARLOW, JILL, ed. *A calendar of the registers of apprentices of the City of Gloucester 1595-1700.* Gloucestershire Record series **14.** Bristol and Gloucestershire Archaeological Society, 2001.

Appurtenances

A term often found in *deeds, meaning the rights and duties attached to a piece of land, especially manorial land. These might include rights of common, rights of way, the duty to appear at manorial courts or to serve in manorial offices, *etc.*

Archdeacon / Archdeaconry

An archdeacon is the person appointed by a bishop to exercise the latter's authority over an archdeaconry, which is a group of parishes within his diocese. His jurisdiction usually included probate, and consequently the first place to look for *wills may be amongst the records of the archdeaconry. Other records which may be of interest to the genealogist are those of archdeacons' visitations and the judicial records of archdeaconry courts.

Further Reading:

- WEBB, C.C., & SMITH, DAVID M. 'Archdeacons records', in THOMPSON, K.M., ed. *Short guide to records. Second series, guides 25-48.* Historical Association, 1997, 38-43.

Archives

Archives are primary sources of information for genealogists, although the latter must realise that they were not created to help him. They are original documents resulting from administrative action which were originally preserved because of their potential use to their owner. They may have been created by central or local government, by an ecclesiastical institution, a company, an estate, a charity, or some other body. Until the 16th century they were usually written in *Latin on parchment; then paper gradually superseded parchment, and *Latin was finally abolished as the language of the law in 1733. Microfilm and computer files are now replacing paper.

The archives which genealogists need to consult are generally to be found in *record offices. They are unique and, in many cases, fragile, so must be handled with great care. You should consult published sources (see *Books, *Bibliographies, and *Libraries) before you head for the archives. Find out what material from the archives has been published; otherwise, you may subject unique documents to unnecessary wear and tear.

Most record repositories have published guides to their holdings, and their web-sites may also provide valuable information. Some *transcripts or *calendars of original documents may have been published: check the county volumes of Raymond's *British Genealogical library guides* to identify these. There are also likely to be unpublished calendars, lists and indexes in the record office itself. Learn how to use these.

Further reading:

- LUMAS, SUSAN B. *Archives.* Basic facts about ... series. F.F.H.S., 1997.
- KITCHING, CHRISTOPHER. *Archives: the very essence of our heritage.* Phillimore, 1996.

Aristocracy and Nobility

The definition of these terms is fluid. Some would argue that only the *peerage should be included; others would include all armigerous families. The terms are generally linked to possession of a landed estate, and to hereditary descent - although few aristocratic families of the present day can trace their lineage to powerful medieval barons.

Numerous pedigrees of noble families are available in print; many pedigree collections are listed in Stuart Raymond's *English genealogy: a bibliography.* 3rd ed. F.F.H.S., 1996, section 7.

Armiger
   A person entitled to a coat of arms, an *esquire.

Armorial Bearings
   See Achievement

Armory
   The study of *heraldry. The term may also be used for books
   recording the arms of families.

Army
   Until the mid-20th century, Englishmen had always been
   under an obligation to bear arms in defence of the realm.
   Surviving records of the army and the *militia are extensive,
   and are an immensely important source for genealogists.
      The earliest standing force was the New Model Army,
   created by Cromwell during the English Civil War, 1642-9,
   but disbanded in 1660. The British Army as it exists today
   has a continuous history since the time of Charles II (1660-
   85). It should not be confused with the *Militia, a term which
   refers to the entire adult male population in its capacity as a
   fighting force.
      The army consisted of regiments, which were the basis of
   its record-keeping. Initially, infantry regiments were divided
   into battalions and companies, cavalry regiments into
   squadrons. Central control was very loose. By the late 18th
   century, there were in effect four separate armies: the
   regulars, the Board of Ordnance (including the Royal
   Artillery and the Royal Engineers), the *Militia, and the
   *Volunteer forces, which were in effect a private army. Mis-
   management during the Crimean War led to a series of
   reforms in 1855: the Board of Ordnance was abolished and a
   series of specialist Corps - transport, medical, supply, *etc.* -
   were set up. In the late 19th century, the War Office was
   radically reorganized and the structure of regiments greatly
   altered, many being linked to counties. The Haldane reform

of 1907-12 led to the creation of the Imperial General Staff, and the creation of an expeditionary force which was the nucleus of the World War I 'Old Contemptibles'.

Most army records are held at the *Public Record Office. However, the *Army list*, which has been published at least annually since 1754, is widely available in major reference *libraries. The outline of officers careers are easily traced using these volumes. Officers' records at the *Public Record Office relate to the purchase of commissions (which continued until 1871), retirement on half-pay, returns of officers services, *etc.*

Soldiers documents (WO97) are the best sources for tracing other ranks; they cover the period 1760-1913. Prior to 1882 they only relate to *Chelsea pensioners. These documents provide information on age, physical appearance, birthplace, and occupation on enlistment, together with a record of service.

Pay lists and muster rolls (WO10-12 & 14-16) require more work from the genealogist, but provide details of soldiers' entire careers in the 18th and 19th centuries. They were compiled by regiment, and provide details of the whereabouts and pay of each soldier.

For the first world war, unfortunately, only a small percentage of army service records survived the Blitz. As a consequence, the authorities had to make a collection of information on soldiers held by the Ministry of Pensions. Their collection is often referred to as the 'Unburnt Records' (WO364) and is the first source to check for information on other ranks. Some 'burnt documents' do survive; these are badly damaged and are being released on microfilm only.

World War I officers may be traced in the *Army lists* mentioned above. Records of service are available in WO339 and WO373.

Personal records of both officers and other ranks post-1920 are still held by the Ministry of Defence, and details will only be given to next of kin.

Army (*continued*)

A wide variety of other records are available; if you have soldier ancestors (and the probability is that you do) you should consult the books listed below.

Many leaflets relating to army records are available on the Public Record Office website at **www.pro.gov.uk/leaflets/Riindex.asp** Records for the First World War, other than those in the Public Record Office, are listed in Holding's *Locations.*

Further Reading:

- FOWLER, SIMON, & SPENCER, WILLIAM, *Army records for family historians.* Public Record Office readers guide **2.** 2nd ed. 1998.
- WATTS, MICHAEL J., & WATTS, CHRISTOPHER T. *My ancestor was in the British Army.* Society of Genealogists, 1995.
- HOLDING, NORMAN. *World War I army ancestry.* 3rd ed. F.F.H.S., 1997.
- HOLDING, NORMAN. *More sources of World War I army ancestry.* 3rd ed. F.F.H.S., 1998.
- HOLDING, NORMAN. *The location of British army records 1914-1918.* ed. Iain Swinnerton. 4th ed. F.F.H.S., 1999.
- *Using army records.* Pocket guides to family history. Public Record Office, 2000.

Many other books could be listed here, but they can easily be found by consulting the foregoing.

Assize Courts

From the early fourteenth century until 1971, the Assize courts were the principal criminal courts in England. They also had a civil jurisdiction. They met twice a year in each county, and dealt with both cases sent up from *Quarter sessions, and with cases referred to them by the central courts. Gaol books, indictments, depositions, and various other documents related to Assize proceedings are in the

*Public Record Office, although survival is patchy, and rare prior to the mid-sixteenth century. A number of calendars of assize records for the Home Circuit have been edited by Cockburn, in addition to the volumes listed below. With the exception of the published records, it is difficult to use Assize files, although they do contain much information of interest to the family historian.

Web Page:
- Assizes: Criminal Trials
  catalogue.pro.gov.uk/Leaflets/ri2231.htm

Further Reading:
- COCKBURN, J. S. *A history of English assizes. 1558-1714.* Cambridge University Press, 1972.
- COCKBURN, J. S. *Calendar of Assize records: Home Circuit indictments. Elizabeth I and James I: Introduction.* H.M.S.O., 1985.
- BARNES, THOMAS G., ed. *Somerset Assize orders 1629-1640.* Somerset Record Society **65.** 1959.
- JOHNSON, D. A., ed. *Staffordshire Assize calendars 1842-1843.* Collections for a history of Staffordshire, 4th series, **15.** Staffordshire Record Society, 1992.

Association Oath Rolls
A Jacobite plot to assassinate William III resulted in the Act of Association 1695/6, which required all office-holders to take a solemn oath to associate with others to defend the King. In practice, most men of any social standing took the oath; their names are listed in the Association Oath rolls, held at the Public Record Office in class C213.

Further Reading:
- GANDY, WALLACE. *The Association Oath rolls of A.D.1696.* Wallace Gandy, 1921.
- GIBSON, J.S.W. *The hearth tax, other late Stuart tax lists, and the Association Oath rolls.* 2nd ed. F.F.H.S., 1996.

Association of Genealogists and Researchers in Archives

A.G.R.A. is the professional body for *professional genealogists; its members are experienced and are required to conform to a code of practice. If you want to pay someone to undertake research on your behalf, you should make sure that the person concerned is a member. The code of practice, and a list of members, is available on the internet.

Web Page:
- Associaton of Genealogists and Researchers in Archives **www.agra.org.uk**

Augmentations

See Court of Augmentations

Australia

The first English colony in Australia was the penal settlement in Botany Bay, founded in 1792. Free settlers first arrived in 1793. It was not until 1901 that the six colonies came together to form the Commonwealth of Australia; consequently all 19th century records will be found in the state archive offices rather than the Australian Archives. Extensive convict records are held by State Records New South Wales. Many have been microfilmed for its *Genealogical research kit*, but, unfortunately, this does not seem to be available in English libraries. The Australian Joint Copying Project has microfilmed extensive records relevant to Australia in English record offices; the microfilms are available in major Australian research libraries, and its *handbooks* enable you to locate the original documents in England.

Civil registration began at various dates in the different states - 1838 in Tasmania, but not until 1930 for the Australian Capital Territory. Most state registries have published indexes to their records on fiche or CD. Census records are scarce, although a few pre-1841 censuses have been published and / or are available at the *Public Record Office, Kew (HO 10/21-7). Probate records are to be found in the custody of probate registries in each state; many have been indexed. Passenger lists can be found in state archives offices.

Most state libraries have good genealogical collections; some include much of interest to English researchers. The libraries of the state genealogical societies are also useful. There are numerous Australian family history societies; their web-sites are listed on Cyndi's List.

Web Pages:

- Cyndi's List: Australia & New Zealand
  www.cyndislist.com/austnz.htmSocieties

- Australian Family History Compendium
  www.cohsoft.com.au/afhc

- Australian Joint Copying Project
  www.nla.gov.au/collect/ajcp.html

Further Reading:

- VINE HALL, NICK. *Tracing your family history in Australia: a guide to sources.* 3rd ed. Albert Park: N. Vine Hall, 2002.
- HAWKINGS, D. *Bound for Australia.* Chichester: Phillimore / Sydney: Library of Australian History, 1987.
- SHEEHAN, C. *The Australian Joint Copying Project for family historians.* Brisbane: Library Board of Queensland, 1987.

B

Bankrupts and Insolvent Debtors

Debtors unable or unwilling to pay their creditors were liable to imprisonment until 1869. Papers relating to them are to be found amongst the records of *Quarter sessions; many are listed in Jeremy Gibson's *Quarter sessions records for family historians: a select list.* 4th ed. F.F.H.S., 1995 Some records may also be found in the *Public Record Office, especially amongst the records of the Fleet and other London prisons (PRIS 1-11), and the archives of the Palace Court (PALA1-9), which had jurisdiction over small debts in the London area. In 1813, the Court for the relief of insolvent debtors was established; petitions to it are in class B1.

Traders who owed over £100 (£50 after 1842) could avoid imprisonment by being made bankrupt. The records of bankruptcy commissioners survive in the *Public Record Office from 1710. Some 19th century bankruptcy records are held in *county record offices. The *London gazette* published notices concerning bankruptcy proceedings, as did the *Times*. There were a number of reforms of bankruptcy law in the 19th century, which affected the prservation of records; further details are given on the Public Record Office web-pages listed below.

Web Pages:

- Bankruptcy petitions after 1869
  catalogue.pro.gov.uk/Leaflets/ri2224.htm

- Bankrupts and Insolvent Debtors 1710-1869
  catalogue.pro.gov.uk/Leaflets/ri2223.htm

Banns

In 1215, the Lateran Council required prospective marriage partners to give notice of their intention to marry by having banns proclaimed in their respective parish churches for three Sundays before the marriage. Banns could, however, be dispensed with by obtaining amarriage licence.

In 1753 Hardwicke's *Marriage Act required the keeping of banns registers; these ceased to be required after *Rose's Act 1812. Unfortunately, few banns registers survive.

Baptism

The rite of baptism - the ritual washing away of sins - is the point at which the person baptised is welcomed into membership of the church. The earliest baptisms were those of adults; however, in the last millenium most babies were baptised soon after birth - rarely more than two weeks; hence the entries for baptisms in *parish registers provide a rough indication of dates of birth. See however, *Baptists. Infant baptism is completed by the rite of confirmation, when the confirmee confirms the vows which were made on his behalf when he was baptised. Some churches - especially the *Roman Catholics - kept confirmation registers, which may be useful to the genealogist.

Baptists

Baptists insist upon the necessity of adult baptism (and sometimes on full immersion). Consequently, registers of Baptist baptisms cannot be used to determine dates of birth. The Baptist church in England emerged from the religious upheavals of the 17th century. As is the case with other nonconformist groups, they underwent various splits, and in particular, lost many churches to the Unitarians in the 18th century. Most churches are now members of the Baptist Union of Great Britain. Many of their early registers are kept with other *Nonconformist registers at the *Public Record Office in RG4. Others are to be found in *county record offices *etc.*, a full list is given in Breed.

Further Reading:

* BREED, GEOFFREY R. *My ancestors were Baptists.* 4th ed. Society of Genealogists, 2002.

Baptists (*continued*)
- 'The three denominations: the Presbyterians (including Unitarians), Independants (or Congregationalists) and Baptists', in STEEL, D. J. *Sources for nonconformist genealogy and family history.* National index of parish registers **2**. Society of Genealogists 1973, 519-600.

Barnardo Homes

T. J. Barnardo founded his first orphanage in Stepney in 1870. The archives of the Homes he established include details of almost all the 350,000 children who have passed through their doors, including photographs. The archives are held at the University of Liverpool, where records over 100 years old may be consulted by arrangement.

Webpage:
- Barnardo's History
  www.barnardos.org.uk/AboutBarnardos/History/index.html

Baron

The lowest rank of the peerage, not to be confused with a *Court Baron.

Baronet

A baronet holds an honorific title first sold by James I in 1611, in order to raise money to pay his troops in Ulster. A baronetcy could be purchased for £1095. A baronet is not of peerage rank.

Bastardy

Bastardy has and had serious financial implications, which is fortunate for the genealogist, if for no-one else. Given that the usual entry for the baptism of a bastard in a parish register only gave the names of the mother and child, other documents are needed to establish the name of the father. Step forward the parish overseer of the poor! He would try to establish the name of the father in order to make him pay for the child's maintainance. Frequently, the parents would marry - although the marriage of an unmarried mother does not necessarily identify the father. If this did not happen, the mother, if she was likely to 'fall on the parish' would be questioned as to paternity; the father would be required to enter into a bond to pay maintainance, and the resultant bastardy bond would be filed in the parish chest. If the father refused, *Quarter sessions would be asked to make a maintainance order, a copy of which would remain with its archives.

The *churchwardens also had the power to present the mother, and the father, if known, before a church court. The court could require the performance of penance; its judgement would be recorded in its archives.

Further Reading:
• McLAUGHLIN, EVE. *Illegitimacy.* 4th ed. F.F.H.S., 1989.

Bernau Index
This is a microfilmed collection of c.4,500,000 slips providing a surname index to various record classes in the *Public Record Office, and especially to *Chancery and *Exchequer court depositions and proceedings.

Further Reading:
• SHARP, HILARY. *How to use the Bernau index.* 2nd ed. Society of Genealogists, 2000.

Bibliography
Bibliographies are frequently ignored by genealogists, but should be one of the first ports of call for any inquiry. A bibliography is, quite simply, a list of *books (and, nowadays, *microfiche, *CD's, *etc.*) arranged in a way which will help you to know what has been published on any given subject. That information is vital to the researcher; it could save a lot of time, and also needless wear and tear on unique and irreplaceable manuscripts. For example, many parish registers have been printed; a bibliography will provide details of them. You may need to consult other records from

Bibliography (*continued*)

the parish chest: bibliographies will identify the books you need to read before looking at the documents, and will also tell you if any relevant documents have been published. You will certainly want to know if anyone has published any research on your ancestors: bibliographies will tell you.

The major series of genealogical bibliographies currently available are Stuart Raymond's *British genealogical library guides* (formerly published as the *British genealogical bibliographies* series). The flagship of this series is *English genealogy: a bibliography* 3rd ed. F.F.H.S., 1996. This volume is intended to be read in conjunction with the county volumes (which do not include material of national interest). Counties covered so far include: Buckinghamshire, Cheshire, Cornwall, Cumberland & Westmorland, Devon, Dorset, Essex, Gloucestershire, Hampshire, Kent, Lancashire, Lincolnshire, London & Middlesex, Norfolk, Oxfordshire, Somerset, Suffolk, Surrey and Sussex, Wiltshire and Yorkshire. These volumes follow a uniform pattern, listing books, journal articles, fiche, CDs, *etc.* on a very wide range of topics - history, bibliography, archives and libraries, journals and newspapers, names, biographical dictionaries, occupational sources, pedigrees, family histories, parish and non-conformist registers, probate records, monumental inscriptions, lists of names, directories, ecclesiastical records, estate and family papers, governmental archives, education, emigration, *etc., etc.* They enable you to conduct a systematic search of published materials without wasting time.

Further Reading:

• RAYMOND, STUART A. *Using Libraries: Workshops for family historians* F.F.H.S., 2001.

A number of bibliographies listing current publications are also available; these include:

• HAMPSON, ELIZABETH. *Current publications by member societies.* 10th ed. F.F.H.S., 1999.

- RAYMOND, STUART A. *British genealogical books in print.* F.F.H.S., 1999.
- PERKINS, JOHN. *Current publications on microfiche by member societies.* 5th ed. F.F.H.S., 2002.
- RAYMOND, STUART A. *British genealogical microfiche.* F.F.H.S., 1999.

Bigamy

The crime of marrying when one is already married. It is likely that this was much more common before 1857, when it became possible to obtain a *divorce.

Biographical Dictionaries

Biographical dictionaries provide brief biographies of millions of people. The best known, and probably the most extensive is the *Dictionary of national biography,* which may be found in most public libraries. Your local reference library is likely to have many similar works covering a wide diversity of subjects, places and periods. Over 16,000 biographical dictionaries are listed in:

- SLOCUM, R. B. *Biographical dictionaries and related works: an international bibliography ...* 2nd ed. Gale Research, 1986.

Many of the dictionaries listed by Slocum are indexed in:

- *Biography and genealogy master index: a consolidated index to more than 3,200,000 biographical sketches in over 350 current and retrospective biographical dictionaries.* 8 vols. Gale, 1980. Supplements 1981-5, 1986-90, and annually from 1991. Also available on CD.

Some 324 of the most important British dictionaries have been microfilmed, and are available in major reference *libraries as:

- *British biographical archive.* 1060 fiche. Saur, 1990. Many other biographical dictionaries are listed in the various volumes of Raymond's *British genealogical library guides.* (See above, *Bibliography).

Biographies

Libraries are full of biographies, which are probably almost as popular as novels for light reading. The family historian will want to read any biographies of family members that may have been published. In addition to the intrinsic interest of the biographee's life, it is likely that genealogical details will be included, and a full family tree may well be found. A number of bibliographies of biographies are available;

The most important are:

- McCOLVIN, L. R. *The librarian's subject guide to books. Vol. 2. Biography, family history, genealogy etc.* James Clarke & Co., 1960.
- *Bibliography of biography 1970-1984.* 40 fiche. British Library, 1985.
- *Biography index: a cumulative index to biographical material in books and magazines.* H. W. Wilson, 1946- .
- *International bibliography of biography 1970-1987.* 12 vols. K. G. Saur, 1988.

It is worth checking the catalogues of major institutions such as the *British Library and the *Library of Congress under the surname(s) sought for details of any biographies that may be available. See also *Biographical Dictionaries.

Birth Certificates

See Civil Registration

Births

Records of births are invaluable sources for family historians, and survive in considerable quantity. *Parish registers (with *bishops' transcripts and *nonconformist registers) and *civil registration records are the most obvious and extensive sources, but there are a variety of other records which may give clues. For example, *census returns give ages and (for most years) place of birth; *Poor Law records such as overseers accounts and settlement examinations often give clues to birth-places and dates;

inquisitions post mortem record the ages of heirs. Various transcripts and indexes to birth registers available on the internet are listed in:
* RAYMOND, STUART A. *Births, marriages and deaths on the web: a directory.* 2 vols. F.F.H.S., 2002.

Bishops/Archbishops Registers

Bishops' registers are the formal records of matters dealt with by bishops, including legal disputes, tithes, church fabric, endowments of ecclesiastical establishments, ordination and supervision of the clergy, wills, and especially the institution of parochial incumbents. Many medieval registers have been published by the Canterbury and York Society, and by other record societies; these are listed in *Texts and calendars.*

Further Reading:
* ROBINSON, DAVID. 'Bishops registers' in THOMPSON, K. M. *Short guides to records. Second series, guides 25-48.* Historical Association, 1997, 44-9.
* SMITH, D. M. *Guide to bishops registers of England and Wales: a survey from the middle ages to the abolition of episcopacy in 1646.* Royal Historical Society, 1981.
* JACOB, E. F., ed. *The register of Henry Chichele, Archbishop of Canterbury, 1414-1443.* 4 vols. Oxford: Clarendon Press, 1938-47. This includes a volume of wills.

Bishops' Transcripts

A transcript of the previous year's parish register entries was sent to the bishop annually, usually at Easter. This practice began in a few dioceses in the mid-sixteenth century, but was made general in 1598. Bishops' transcripts may now be found in diocesan record offices. However, there are gaps in most series, and the original entries in registers were not always carefully copied - although, on the odd occasion, they may actually yield more information than the register: some clergy completed the register at the same time as the transcript, and may have filled them in differently.

Bishops' Transcripts (*continued*)

Many county record offices have published lists of their holdings, and these should be consulted. The county volumes of the *National index of parish registers* (published by the Society of Genealogists) indicates what transcripts are available for each parish.

Further Reading:
- GIBSON, J. *Bishops transcripts and marriage licences; bonds and allegations: a guide to their location and indexes.* 5th ed. F.F.H.S., 2001.

Blazon
A technical description of arms, worded so that they may be accurately painted.

Blue Books
Popular name for *Parliamentary papers.

Boards of Guardians
Boards of guardians were established under the New Poor Law Act 1834. The boards were locally elected in order to administer the *Poor Law in 'unions' of parishes. Initially, they ran the workhouses where paupers received relief, but they subsequently acquired other responsibilities, including *civil registration, rating, school attendance and child protection. They were abolished in 1930.The records of the Guardians are extensive, including minutes, workhouse admission and discharge registers, registers of workhouse births, baptisms, deaths and burials (not marriages!), correspondence, *apprenticeship records, *accounts (including payments to paupers to emigrate), personnel records, reports, *etc., etc.* Most people in nineteenth-century England lived in fear of the workhouse, and it is quite likely that you have ancestors recorded in the archives of the Guardians.

Further Reading:
- GIBSON, JEREMY, *et al. Poor law union records.* 2nd ed. 4 vols. F.F.H.S., 1997-2000.

- COLEMAN, JANE M. 'Guardians minute books', in MUNBY, L. M., ed. *Short guides to records. First series, 1-24.* Historical Association, 1994, 37-40.

Bodleian Library

The library of the University of Oxford was founded by Sir Thomas Bodley in 1598. It is entitled to receive a copy of every book published in the United Kingdom, and is therefore, a rich resource for family historians. Many of the major county journals and *record society publications are available on open access in Duke Humfrey's Library; most other books are housed in closed access stacks, so you will need to use *bibliographies to identify the *books you need before requesting them via the catalogue. The Bodleian also holds an extensive collection of *archives and *manuscripts, including, for example, numerous *deeds, *wills proved in the University Chancellor's court, *estate records, *etc., etc.* Admission is by readers ticket, which non-members of the university must pay for. A referee is required, and new members must swear an oath not to deface or remove books.

Web Page:
- Bodleian Library
  www.bodley.ox.ac.uk

Further Reading:
- TOMLINSON, S. R. 'The Bodleian Library and the genealogist', *Genealogists magazine* **22**, 1987, 277-82.
- HASSALL, W.O., *Index of persons in Oxfordshire deeds acquired by the Bodleian Library 1878-1963.* Oxfordshire Record Society **45**. 1966.

Bond

A bond was a legal document requiring the performance of a particular action. It is written in two parts: the obligation (in Latin prior to 1733), recording the penalty for non-performance, and the condition, which states the action required to prevent the penalty being inflicted.

Bond (*continued*)

Bonds were used for a variety of purposes. An
*administration bond was required before letters of
administration for a deceased persons' estate could be
granted. *Marriage licences required the parties to enter a
bond. Many bonds are mentioned in *probate inventories,
where they are securities for debt.

Books

Books are essential tools for genealogists. They provide
invaluable guidance for both beginners and more experienced
researchers; they contain a huge mass of information from
the *archives, making the latter far more accessible; they are
the means by which many genealogists publish their family
histories. All this may seem so obvious that it is not worth
saying - were it not for the fact that so often their
importance is ignored, and that so often genealogists fail to
check out what is in print before going to the archives.

Every genealogist needs to continually check
*bibliographies as research progresses, to find out whether
any information on the particular points being investigated
is in print. It is a fact that perhaps 30% of questions asked
on internet newsgroups could be answered by checking
bibliographies and then finding the relevant book.

Books can be consulted in several ways. *Libraries maintain
vast collections which are readily accessible; they may also
be able to borrow books on inter-library loan. *Local studies
libraries are particularly useful to the genealogist, since they
generally aim to collect everything published in their area.

Books can also be purchased. Bookshops (and libraries)
are able to check the availability of particular titles. If the
book you want is out of print, it may be available second-
hand - so check the second-hand sites on the web listed
below. Most *family history societies have bookstalls, and
also publish many transcripts and indexes of original
sources as *books, *microfiche and *CDs. Many of them have

stands on *Genfair, the internet's virtual genealogical fair. The *Society of Genealogists and the *Federation of Family History Societies both have extensive on-line bookshops. Commercial organisations such as *Family Tree Magazine* and the present author's Internet Genealogical Bookshop may also be able to help. Many older works are now available on CD.

A third possibility is that you may be able to obtain the help of another genealogist who owns or has access to the book you need to consult. Internet *mailing lists may be used to make contact; there are also a number of dedicated look-up sites.

Web Sites:

- Family History Books, from the Federation of Family History Societies
  www.ffhs.co.uk/
- Society of Genealogists Bookshop On-line UK
  www.sog.org.uk/acatalog/index.html
- Genfair
  www.genfair.com
- Family Tree Magazine
  www.family-tree.co.uk
- Internet Genealogical Bookshop
  www.samjraymond.btinternet.co.uk/igb.htm
- Bibliofind
  www.bibliofind.com
  Second-hand books
- UK Book World
  ukbookworld.com
  Second-hand books
- Books We Own List
  www.rootsweb.com/~bwo/index.html
- The Look-Up Exchange
  www.geocities.com/Heartland/Plains/8555/lookup.html

Border Marriages

Lord Hardwicke's *marriage act, 1753, which came into force in 1754, required all marriages to be performed in a licensed building. In Scotland, all that was required was consent to marriage in the presence of witnesses. Consequently eloping couples made for Gretna Green or one of the other places just over the Border where businesses could provide the necessary witnesses.

Borough English

That system of inheritance under which the youngest son inherited his father's estate.

Boroughs

Between the medieval period and the twentieth century many towns and villages were incorporated as boroughs, and gained a variety of local government powers. In some places these even included the right to hold their own *Quarter Sessions. Consequently, their archives frequently include much of interest to genealogists. Council minutes and order books, the accounts of chamberlains and other officers, *estate records for borough properties, records of courts - the mayor's court, the manorial court leet, the court of orphans, quarter sessions - lists of *freemen, apprenticeship registers, *etc., etc.,* all may yield valuable clues to the genealogist.

Further Reading:

- WEST, JOHN. *Town records.* Phillimore, 1983.
- GROSS, CHARLES. *A bibliography of British municipal history, including gilds and Parliamentary representation.* 2nd ed. Leicester University Press, 1966. Continued by:
- MARTIN, G.H., & McINTYRE, SYLVIA. *Bibliography of British and Irish municipal history, volume 1: General works.* Leicester University Press, 1972.
- DOBSON, R. B., ed. *York City chamberlains' account rolls 1396-1500.* Surtees Society **192**. 1980.

- POWER, MICHAEL, ed. *Liverpool town books 1649-1671.*
  Record Society of Lancashire and Cheshire **136**. 1999.
- RATHBONE, MAURICE G. *List of Wiltshire borough
  records earlier in date than 1836.* Wiltshire
  Archaeological and Natural History Society records
  branch **5**. 1949.

Borthwick Institute of Historical Research

The Borthwick is a department of York University, and
specializes in the ecclesiastical history of the Northern
Province, i.e. the Archdiocese of York. It houses the York
Diocesan archives, including parish registers, probate
records, bishops transcripts, ecclesiastical court records, *etc.
etc.*

Web Page:
- Borthwick Institute of Historical Research
  www.york.ac.uk/inst/bihr/

Further Reading:
- WEBB, C. C. *A guide to genealogical sources in the
  Borthwick Institute of Historical Research.* 1981.
- SMITH, D. M. *A guide to the archive collections in the
  Institute of Historical Research.* Borthwick texts and
  calendars: records of the Northern Province **1**. 1973.
  Supplement 1980.

Boyds Marriage Index

This indexes entries in the published marriage registers of 16
counties in various parts of England pre-1837. It is available
for searching at the *Society of Genealogists and also
(partially) the *Guildhall Library; it is now also becoming
available on-line.

Web Page:
- Boyds Marriage Index 1538-1840
  www.englishorigins.com/help/bmi-details.aspx

Further Reading:
- *A list of parishes in Boyds marriage index.* Library sources **3.** 6th ed. Society of Genealogists 1994.

Brasses
Memorial brasses were introduced into England in the 13th century; they usually commemorate the wealthier members of the community.

Web Pages:
- Monumental Brasses on the Internet
  www.medievalgenealogy.org.uk/sources/brasses.shtml

- Monumental Brass Society
  www.mbs-brasses.co.uk

Further Reading:
- STEPHENSON, M. *A list of monumental brasses in the British Isles.* Headley Brothers, 1926.
- GRIFFIN, R. *Appendix to a list of monumental brasses in the British Isles by Mill Stephenson.* Headley Brothers, 1938.
- PAGE-PHILLIPS, J. *Macklin's monumental brasses.* 2nd ed. George Allen & Unwin, 1972.

British Association for Local History
The B.A.L.H. was founded in 1962 to promote the interests of local historians at the national level. Its journal, the *Local historian,* includes many useful articles on methodology, and is the leading journal in its field. The Association also publishes various handbooks, together with *Local history news.*

Web Page:
- British Association for Local History
  www.balh.com

British Isles

The British Isles is a geographical term encompassing the
United Kingdom of Great Britain and Northern Ireland, the
Republic of Eire, the Channel Islands, and the Isle of Man.

British Isles Genealogical Register (Big-R)

The 2000 edition of the Big-R lists almost 200,000 surnames
currently being researched, giving contact addresses for the
10,000+ researchers who have submitted entries.

British Library

The British Library is second only to the Library of
Congress in the extent of its collections. It is legally entitled
to a copy of every book published in the United Kingdom. Its
genealogical collections are probably superior to those of any
other UK library, although it has not collected genealogical
microfiche or CD's to any great extent. Its book catalogue is
now available on-line, although its printed catalogue,
available in most major reference libraries, remains worth
consulting for *family histories and for publications relating
to particular places and institutions. This catalogue has
many peculiarities useful to genealogists; particularly useful
headings include 'England: Army', 'Directories', and 'England:
College of Arms'. It should be checked by all genealogists; in
addition to being the British Library's catalogue, it also
functions as a *bibliography - a guide to books which may
also be found in many other libraries.

The British Library also holds extensive manuscript
collections, including much material of genealogical interest,
deeds, diaries, pedigrees, *etc., etc.* It also holds an extensive
collection of *newspapers. See also *Oriental & India Office
Collections.

Admission is by readers ticket, available at the library; you
must be able to demonstrate that the material you need to
consult is not easily available elsewhere.

Web Page:
- British Library
  www.bl.uk

Further Reading:
- *The British Library general catalogue of printed books to 1975.* 360 vols + 6 supplementary vols. Clive Bingley, 1979-87. Some libraries may have an earlier edition.
- NICKSON, M. A. E. *The British Library: guide to the catalogues and indexes of the Department of Manuscripts.* 2nd ed. British Library, 1982.

British Record Society
Publishers of the *Index Library.

Brother
Sometimes used to mean brother-in-law.

Burial Indexes
Many family history societies and others have compiled burial indexes - which may be indexes to *parish registers, *monumental inscriptions, cemetery records, *etc.*. Those which have been published, whether as booklets or fiche, are listed in the county volumes of Raymond's *British genealogical library guides,* and in the other volumes mentioned under *Bibliography. Unpublished indexes may be located in two works:
- GIBSON, JEREMY, & HAMPSON, ELIZABETH. *Specialist indexes for family historians.* 2nd ed. F.F.H.S., 2000.
- JONES, BRIAN. *Index of indexers.* 6 pts. to date. Brian Jones, 1994-2001.

Many family history societies have recently pooled their resources to publish an index on CD listing over 5,000,000 names from throughout the country:
- *National burial index.* CD. F.F.H.S., 2001.

Burial Registers

Burial registers are primarily to be found in *parish registers, and in the records of *Civil Registration. However, they were also kept by Boards of Guardians, and by cemetery authorities. Early registers of some of the latter are now in the *Public Record Office (RG4); others remain with cemeteries or are deposited in *county record offices. The Public Record Office also holds many registers of overseas deaths.

Various transcripts and indexes of burial registers on the internet are listed in:
* RAYMOND, STUART A. *Births, Marriages and Deaths on the web: a directory.* 2 vols. F.F.H.S., 2002.

Business Records

Businesses have shareholders, employees and customers; information about all three groups may be found in their records. Registers of share-holders, lists of directors, personnel records, pay-lists, *etc.,* may all provide information about your ancestor.

The location of business records is probably best checked by consulting the National Register of Archives. Names and addresses of shareholders and directors may be found amongst the records which had to be filed with the Registrar of Companies, a few of which are now in the *Public Record Office, which also has some records of companies which have been nationalised.

Web Pages:
* Business Archives Council
  www.archives.gla.ac.uk/bac/default.html

* National Register of Archives: Sources for Business History
  www.hmc.gov.uk/business/busarchives.htm

Further Reading:
* PROBERT, E.D. *Company and business records for family historians.* F.F.H.S., 1994.

- ARMSTRONG, J., & JONES, S. *Business documents: their origins, sources and uses in historical research.* Mansell, 1987.

By-Names

Since medieval times, by-names have been used to distinguish individuals with the same forename. They were particularly common before the introduction of hereditary *surnames. This practice continued even as late as the twentieth century. A by-name might be a nick-name, a place, an occupation, or perhaps a father's name. By-names were liable to change, depending on circumstances, but many became hereditary surnames, sometimes replacing previous surnames.

C

Cadet Branch
 The junior branch of a family.

Calendar
 This word has two entirely different meanings for the
 genealogist:

 1. The calculation of time is normally done by means of a
    calendar. See *Dates.
 2. An archivist's term, indicating a listing of documents
    which summarises the information contained in them, and
    normally including all personal and place-names. Many
    have been published - but, be warned - the matters you
    consider important may not have been considered to be of
    any significance by the compiler, and may therefore not be
    noted.

C.A.M.P.O.P.
 The Cambridge Group for the History of Population and
 Social Structure were the first to use *parish registers
 systematically to study historical demography. The Group
 holds a large quantity of historical demographic data in
 machine-readable form - including much information drawn
 from parish registers.

 • The Cambridge Group for the History of Population and
   Social Structure
   www-hpss.geog.cam.ac.uk/

Canada
 The earliest European settlements in what is now Canada
 were those of the French in Quebec, the English in

Canada (*continued*)

Newfoundland, and the trading posts of the Hudsons Bay Company. By 1763, all of eastern Canada was under British control, and settlement began to spread westwards. However, it was not until 1867 that the various provinces began to come together to form the Dominion of Canada, and it was not until 1949 that the process of confederation was completed: Newfoundland and Labrador were the last colonies to become Canadian provinces. For the genealogist, this history means that many of the records needed are to be found in provincial archives rather than in the National Archives. It also means that civil registration is not uniform, and commencement dates vary from province to province - the latest is 1926 in Quebec. Decennial Census records are available at the dominion level from 1871; a few earlier returns are extant for particular provinces. The National Archives of Canada hold many *passenger lists, invaluable for tracing English emigrants.

Further Reading:
- BAXTER, ANGUS. *In search of your Canadian roots: tracing your family tree in Canada.* 3rd ed. Baltimore: Genealogical Publishing, 2000.

Cantref

An early Welsh administrative area, now obsolete, similar to the English hundred.

Cartulary

A cartulary (or chartulary) is a register of the *deeds and *charters *etc.* of a particular estate - usually, but not exclusively, monastic. Many are held by the *Public Record Office, the *British Library, and other repositories; quite a few have been published by *record societies and other publishers.

Web Page:
- Cartularies
  www.le.ac.uk/elh/pot/char/cart.html

Further Reading:
- DAVIS, G. R. C. *Medieval cartularies of Great Britain: a short catalogue.* Longmans, Green & Co., 1958.
- HOCKEY, S. F., ed. *The Beaulieu cartulary.* Southampton records series **17.** 1974.
- HULL, P. L., ed. *The cartulary of Launceston Priory.* Devon and Cornwall Record Society New series **30.** 1987.

Catholic Record Society

This society has published many original *Roman Catholic sources including registers of baptisms, marriages and burials, and many recusant rolls. A full list of its publications can be found in *Texts and Calendars,* and on the society's web page.

Web Page:
- Catholic Record Society
  www.catholic-history.org.uk/crs/

Further Reading:
- GOOCH, L., *A descriptive catalogue of the publications of the Catholic Record Society 1904-1989.* Catholic Record Society, 1990.

CD's

The last few years have seen an explosion in the publication of genealogical information on CD. At least 1,500 genealogical CD's are currently available from over 70 different publishers, mostly commercial organizations, although a few *family history societies are now becoming involved. By the time you read this there are likely to be many more. Most of these CD's make available books which have long been out of print - especially *trade directories and published *parish registers. Very few contain material compiled specifically for publication on CD - although those few are mostly of major importance, eg. the F.F.H.S's *National burial index.* There are also a handful of CD's

CDs (*continued*)

containing images of original sources. The full potentiality of the format for family historians has yet to be realised. Very few libraries collect genealogical CD's, apart from a handful of *family history societies. There is a growing collection at the *Society of Genealogists, but no library has a comprehensive collection.

Web Pages:

- Archive CD Books Project
  www.archivecdbooks.com/indexes/

- S & N Genealogy Supplies
  www.genealogy.demon.co.uk

Further Reading:

- RAYMOND, STUART A. *British Family History on CD.* F.F.H.S., 2001.

Cemeteries

By the nineteenth century, many urban churchyards were full, and unable to accommodate any more burials. In order to deal with the problem, private companies, municipal authorities, and burial boards (created by legislation in the 1850's) established new cemeteries not linked to the churches. Some nonconformist cemeteries had also been established.

The registers of cemeteries established before 1834 are in the *Public Record Office. Later registers may have been deposited in *county record offices, or may remain in the custody of cemetery superintendants. A few *family history societies have published indexes of cemetery records.

Further Reading:

- WOLFSTON, S. *Greater London Cemeteries and Crematoria.* 4th ed., rev. Clifford Webb. Society of Genealogists, 1997.

Census Returns

Lists of names are vital sources for genealogists; the most useful lists are those which encompass the entire population, that is, the census returns. In theory, the census returns currently available to genealogists provide complete listings of the population every ten years between 1841 and 1901. But be aware that mistakes could be, and were, made! The first national census was taken in 1801, but names were not officially recorded before 1841 - although a handful of name lists from earlier censuses may be found in *county record offices (see *Censuses, Local).

The 1841 returns simply list names, sexes, ages, occupations and counties of birth. The genealogist needs to understand that the ages given are only approximate; except in the case of fourteen year olds and under, they are rounded down to the nearest 5 years, i.e. a person aged 39 will be shown as 35.

Subsequent returns include rather more information; in particular, they show the relationship to the household head, and indicate the place of birth (rather than just the county) if in England and Wales.

Census returns are arranged by enumeration districts - normally the parish in rural areas, but in the major cities you need to know addresses in order to find entries quickly. Many *family history societies have compiled census indexes; these are fully listed by Gibson & Hampson; and also in the county volumes of Raymond's *British genealogical library guides*, and on most society websites.

The 1881 census has been fully indexed on microfiche, and is widely available. The 1901 census can be consulted on the internet. Bear in mind, however, that transcription errors do occur when compiling indexes. It is always best to check the original returns, which are now held in the Public Record Office's *Family Records Centre, where they can be consulted on microfiche. Many *county record offices and *local studies libraries also hold microfilm copies of the originals.

Web Pages:
• Census Leaflets
  **www.pro.gov.uk/readers/research/leaflets/
  censusmain.htm**

Census Returns (*continued*)

- 1901 Census Online
  www.pro.gov.uk/census/

- The Census: Genuki Page
  www.genuki.org.uk/big/eng/census.html

Further Reading:

- LUMAS, SUSAN. *Making use of the census.* Public Record Office Readers guide 1. 4th ed., 2002.
- GIBSON, JEREMY, & HAMPSON, ELIZABETH. *Marriage and census indexes for family historians.* 7th ed. F.F.H.S., 1998.
- HIGGS, EDWARD. *A clearer sense of the census: the Victorian censuses and historical research.* Public Record Office handbooks **28.** H.M.S.O., 1996.
- HIGGS, EDWARD. 'Census returns in England and Wales', in THOMPSON, K. M. *Short guides to records. Second series, 26-48.* Historical Association, 1997, 59-62.
- *Using census returns.* Pocket guides to family history. Public Record Office, 2000.

Censuses, Local

Numerous lists of inhabitants have been compiled unofficially, especially by the clergy; these are occasionally to be found in *parish records and elsewhere. A few lists from the pre-1841 censuses may also be found in *county record offices.

Further Reading:

- GIBSON, J. S. W., & MEDLYCOTT, M. *Local census listings 1522-1930: holdings in Great Britain.* 3rd ed. F.F.H.S., 2001.
- CHAPMAN, COLIN R. *Pre-1841 censuses and population listings in the British Isles.* 5th ed. Dursley: Lochin Publishing, 1998.
- BAKER, DAVID, ed. *The inhabitants of Cardington in 1782.* Bedfordshire Historical Record Society **52.** 1973.

Certificates of Residence

Taxpayers were only liable to the *lay subsidy for one place of residence. Those who had more than one residence paid one tax collector, and obtained a certificate of residence from him in order to claim exemption at his other residence(s). Surviving certificates are in the *Public Record Office, class E179 for the reign of Henry VIII, class E115 for Edward VI - Charles II.

Chancery
See Court of Chancery

Changes of Name
Anyone can change their name; they do not, however, necessarily have to officially record such changes. Nevertheless, if proof of a name change is required, evidence may have to be supplied. There are various ways in which this could be done, ranging from a simple newspaper advertisement to an Act of Parliament (the latter method was last used in 1907).

The deed poll is probably the best known method: drawn up by a solicitor, it could be enrolled on the *Close Rolls, although more frequently it was not. An alternative was a statutory declaration made before a J.P. or Commissioner for Oaths. A royal licence was common in the seventeenth-century, although now usually only acquired where a bequest or marriage settlement requires a change of name, or a coat of arms has to be changed. Such changes were frequently advertised in the *London gazette.*

Web Pages:
- Change of Name
  catalogue.pro.gov.uk/Leaflets/ri2250.htm

Further Reading:
- PHILLIMORE, W. P. W., & FRY, E. A. *An index to change of name under authority of act of parliament or royal licence and including irregular changes from 1 George III to 64 Victoria 1760 to 1901.* Phillimore & Co., 1905. Reprinted Baltimore: Genealogical Publishing Co., 1968. This is not intended to be a complete listing of name changes.

Channel Islands

The Channel Islands - Guernsey, Jersey, Alderney, Sark, *etc.,* - are not part of the United Kingdom. Rather, they are the only parts of the Duchy of Normandy still belonging to the English crown, and have their own governments - although defence and foreign affairs are the responsibility of the British government. Consequently, genealogical records in the Channel Islands differ substantially from those in England and Wales. For example, *civil registration of births and deaths began in Guernsey in 1840, in Jersey in 1842, and in Sark and Alderney in 1925. A detailed discussion of Channel Islands genealogical research cannot be provided here; reference should be made to the web-sites and further reading listed below.

Web Sites:

- Channel Islands Genealogy
  www.cigenealogy.co.uk

- Alex Glendinning's Channel Islands Pages
  users.itl.net/~glen/CIintro.html

- Channel Islands Genuki
  user.itl.net/~glen/genuki.html

Further Reading:

- BACKHURST, MARIE-LOUISE. *Family history in Jersey.* Channel Islands Family History Society, 1991.
- LE POIDEVIN, DAVID W. *How to trace your ancestors in Guernsey.* Taunton: Quality Service, 1978.

Chapel/Chapelry

Chapel is a word which may cause some confusion, since it is used for four different buildings: the domestic chapel of a lord, the chapel of ease built to serve parishioners who lived at a distance from the parish church (there were many of them in the north, mostly now elevated to the status of parish churches), the chapel in a parish church which was built to house a side altar, and the nonconformist chapel. A chapelry is the area served by a chapel of ease.

Chapman County Codes

These three-letter codes are widely used by family historians to denote county names in indexes *etc.* They include codes for counties throughout the British Isles, including both pre- and post-1974 counties. A complete list is given on the web-page. The codes for pre-1974 English and Welsh counties are as follows:

AGY	Anglesey	HUN	Huntingdonshire
ALD	Alderney	IOM	Isle of Man
BDF	Bedfordshire	IOW	Isle of Wight
BKM	Buckinghamshire	JST	Jersey
BRE	Brecknockshire	KEN	Kent
BRK	Berkshire	LAN	Lancashire
CAE	Caernarvonshire	LEI	Leicestershire
CAM	Cambridgeshire	LIN	Lincolnshire
CGN	Cardiganshire	LND	London
CHI	Channel Islands	MDX	Middlesex
CHS	Cheshire	MER	Merionethshire
CMN	Carmarthenshire	MGY	Montgomeryshire
CON	Cornwall	MON	Monmouthshire
CUL	Cumberland	NBL	Northumberland
DBY	Derbyshire	NFK	Norfolk
DEN	Denbighshire	NRY	Yorkshire North Riding
DEV	Devon	NTH	Northamptonshire
DOR	Dorset	NTT	Nottinghamshire
DUR	Durham	OXF	Oxfordshire
ERY	Yorkshire East Riding	PEM	Pembrokeshire
ESS	Essex	RAD	Radnorshire
FLN	Flintshire	RUT	Rutland
GLA	Glamorgan	SAL	Shropshire
GLS	Gloucestershire	SFK	Suffolk
GSY	Guernsey	SOM	Somerset
HAM	Hampshire	SRK	Sark
HEF	Herefordshire	SRY	Surrey
HRT	Hertfordshire	SSX	Sussex

STS	Staffordshire	WLS	Wales
WAR	Warwickshire	WOR	Worcestershire
WES	Westmorland	WRY	Yorkshire West Riding
WIL	Wiltshire	YKS	Yorkshire

Web Page:
• Country & County Codes: British Isles
  www.genuki.org.uk/big/Regions/Codes.html

Charities

Until the nineteenth century, most charities were local, and were frequently administered by parish officials. Usually, they were for the benefit of the poor, the binding of apprentices, the founding and/or maintainance of a church or school, and similar purposes. Their records - deeds, rentals, accounts, lists of beneficiaries, *etc.* - mention many names, and may provide invaluable evidence for genealogists. They are frequently to be found in the parish chest.

From 1786, the Clerk of the Peace had to submit their accounts to Parliament, and consequently records may also be found with Quarter Sessions records. The massive *Reports of the Commission for Inquiry concerning Charities* 32 vols. H.M.S.O., 1819-40 was intended to provide a detailed account of every charity in existence, and contains a great deal of information on founders, benefactions and trustees, *etc.* - although not the names of beneficiaries.

Charters and Charter Rolls

A charter is a legal document granting rights, which may be of various sorts, e.g. rights to markets, to lands, to boroughs, *etc.*. The Charter rolls (class C53 in the *Public Record Office) found amongst the records of the *Court of Chancery, and dating from 1199 to 1517, record royal grants of lands, honours and privileges. There are many published transcripts of charters, listed in *Texts and calendars;* a select few are listed below.

Further Reading:

- *Calendar of the charter rolls preserved in the Public Record Office.* 5 vols. H.M.S.O., 1903-16. For 1226-1417.
- FARRER, WILLIAM, ed. *Early Yorkshire charters ...* 3 vols. Edinburgh: Ballantyne Hanson & Co., 1914. Continued by: CLAY, CHARLES TRAVIS. *Early Yorkshire charters.* 9 vols. (i.e. index to Farrer, plus 7 further vols. denominated v's 4-10). Leeds: Yorkshire Archaeological Society, 1935-65.
- GREENWAY, D. E., ed. *Charters of the Honour of Mowbray 1107-1191.* Records of social and economic history N.S. 1. Oxford University Press for the British Academy, 1972.
- BEARMAN, ROBERT, ed. *Charters of the Redvers family and the Earldom of Devon 1090-1217.* Devon and Cornwall Record Society, N.S., **37**. 1994.

Chartulary

See Cartulary

Chatham Chest

The Chatham Chest, as it is popularly known, was established in 1590 to support invalid Royal Naval seamen and dockyard workers and their widows. In 1803, its administration was taken over by the *Royal Greenwich Hospital. Its records, now at the *Public Record Office, include annual lists of pensioners, registers of payments to pensioners, *etc.*

Chattels

Chattels comprise all personal property except land held freehold. *Probate inventories list 'goods and chattels' and frequently list 'chattle leases', i.e. land held by lease, rather than freehold.

Chelsea Pensioners

The Royal Hospital at Chelsea was founded by Charles II in 1681 to care for invalid army pensioners - who consequently became known as Chelsea Pensioners, although the majority were out-pensioners, and did not live at Chelsea. The

Chelsea Pensioners (*continued*)

Hospital's commissioners retained responsibility for the payment of army pensions until 1955. See also *Army.

Web Page:
• British Army Soldiers Pensions (1702-1913)
  catalogue.pro.gov.uk/leaflets/ri2006.htm

Child Migrant Index

This is a government-sponsored database compiled by the National Council of Voluntary Child Care Organisations containing basic information on child migrants sent abroad by U.K. sending agencies. Full details are given on the website at **www.ncvcco.org/projects/childmigrant.htm**

Childrens Societies

The *Barnardo Homes were far from being the only institution concerned with the care of orphans in the nineteenth and early twentieth centuries. Others included, for example, the Shaftesbury Homes (1843), the Thomas Coram Foundation (1739), the National Childrens Home (1869), *etc.* There is no overall guide to the records of these charities; however, reference libraries should be able to trace the addresses of those which still exist. Consultation of the *National Register of Archives, and *A2A, may lead you to the records of defunct institutions.

Christian Names

The history of Christian names reflects the history of England, and is worth studying in its own right as well as for genealogical purposes. Many of the names used today were originally Anglo-Saxon, Norman, or Biblical. The Norman Conquest, unfortunately, resulted in the loss of many Anglo-Saxon names, although some were revived in the nineteenth century. One has been revived by a popular author of the twentieth century - but I do not know any living person named Gandalf! Norman names have been dominant throughout most of England's history: in the fourteenth century, for example, just five names - the names of kings and dukes of Normandy - contributed no less than 64% of recorded masculine names. The popularity of Henry, John, Robert, Richard and William still causes many problems to genealogists faced with identical names. The growth of Puritanism in the seventeenth-century made Biblical names more popular, and also made names such as Faith, Hope, and Charity common; the Tractarian movement in the nineteenth century to some extent revived the use of long neglected saints' names such as Aidan and Ninian.

The names given in documents are frequently abbreviated and in Latin, e.g. Johannes or Jno for John. Steel gives a list of these abbreviations.

The practise of having two or more christian names was virtually unknown before the sixteenth century. This seems to have been a custom originating in southern Europe taken up by the English aristocracy in the seventeenth century.

- 'Christian names', in STEEL, D. J., *et al. Sources of births marriages and deaths before 1837 (I)*. National index of parish registers 1. Society of Genealogists, 1968, 101-28.
- WITHYCOMBE, E. G. *The Oxford dictionary of English christian names*. 3rd ed. Oxford: Clarendon Press, 1977.
- HANKS, PATRICIA, & HODGES, FLAVIA. *A dictionary of first names*. Oxford University Press, 1990.

Church

In popular parlance, the church is a building. The word does however, have a much wider connotation. At its broadest extent, it refers to the whole company of Christian believers, past and present. It may also be used to refer to the church in a particular area, to a denomination, or to a particular church, e.g. the Church in Wales, the Methodist Church, South Street Baptist Church Exeter.

Church Courts

In previous centuries, the church as an institution had much greater influence in the life of society than it does today. In particular, it sought to exercise strict control over morals and beliefs; it had authority over marital issues, and it exercised jurisdiction over probate. All of these matters were dealt with through the church courts, which were distinct from the civil courts. A wide range of ecclesiastical courts existed; in addition to those at the Provincial level, e.g. the *Prerogative Court of Canterbury and the *Court of Arches, each Diocese had its consistory and archidiaconal courts; there might also be *peculiar courts. The records of these courts are of considerable value to genealogists, especially between the sixteenth and the eighteenth centuries; they can be found with the *diocesan records. Unfortunately their cramped *handwriting and scribbled abbreviations make them difficult to use. Records include *act books, citations, libels, depositions, interrogatories, *etc.* Depositions in particular can be very useful, as they provide much information about witnesses.

Further Reading:

- TARVER, ANNE. *Church court records: an introduction for family and local historians.* Chichester: Phillimore & Co., 1995.
- CHAPMAN, COLIN R. *Sin, sex and probate: ecclesiastical courts, officials and records.* Dursley: Lochin Publications, 1997.
- GIESE, LOREEN L., ed. *London Consistory Court depositions 1586-1611: list and indexes.* London Record Society **32**. 1995.
- BOWKER, MARGARET, ed. *An episcopal court book for the Diocese of Lincoln, 1514-1520.* Lincoln Record Society **61**. 1967.

Church of Jesus Christ of Latter-Day Saints

The Latter Day Saints (L.D.S., or Mormons, as they are popularly called) believe that their ancestors can become members of their church by post-mortem baptism - but first they have to be identified. That is the rationale behind the church's enormous investment in genealogy. Their Family History Library in Salt Lake City is the largest library devoted solely to genealogy in the world; it has extensive British collections including innumerable *parish registers on microfilm, which can be accessed from any of its thousands of *Family History Centers, including many in Britain.

The L.D.S. are also responsible for the *_International Genealogical Index_, for the index of the 1881 *census, and for *_Ancestral File_.

Web Pages:
- Family Search
  www.familysearch.org

Further Reading:
- HAWGOOD, DAVID. _Family search on the internet._ F.F.H.S./David Hawgood, 1999.

Church Rates
Church rates could be levied by the *churchwardens on all householders within their parish, regardless of whether they attended church. Rate lists can often be found in the parish chest. This impost was abolished in 1868.

Church Seating
It is not often realised that pews are a relatively recent innovation. In the medieval period, most people stood in the nave during services. The introduction of pews enabled leading parishioners to formalize the social structure of their parish in the seating plan. The owners or tenants of the largest properties sat at the front, smallholders in the middle, and cottagers at the rear. Sometimes, this caused disputes over precedence, and seating plans had to be drawn up in order for a court to make a judgement. Seating plans do not exist for every parish, but where they do they may serve as a census of the entire parish, showing where everyone sat in church. They may be found with *diocesan or *parish records

Churchwardens

Since at least the twelfth century, churchwardens have been the chief lay officers of the parish church. Each parish usually has two wardens, sometimes more in populous parishes. Their method of appointment varied from parish to parish, although frequently the leading inhabitants served by rotation. Their prime duties have always been - and continue to be - the maintainance of church fabric, the administration of church income and property, and the preservation of good order in everything to do with the church. However, many civil duties were added to their responsibilites in the fifteenth and sixteenth centuries, ranging from the relief of the poor to the destruction of vermin. Churchwardens' accounts reflect the wide range of these duties, recording the receipt of income from church properties, from gifts, and from the levying of *church rates, and payments for numerous purposes, ranging from the purchase of pews to payment for dead vermin, from relief of the poor to the dog-whippers wages.

These accounts were not designed with the genealogist in mind, but nevertheless may provide useful evidence. The many names they contain provide proof of the presence of particular people in a particular parish at a particular time. Accounts are normally to be found with other *parish records in *county record offices; a list of extant accounts pre-1690 is given by Hutton, who also lists a number of printed accounts.

Further Reading:

- COX, J. C. *Churchwardens accounts from the fourteenth century to the close of the seventeenth century.* Methuen & Co., 1913
- HUTTON, RONALD. *The rise and fall of merry England: the ritual year 1400-1700.* Oxford University Press, 1994. Includes detailed list of surviving accounts.
- DYMOND, DAVID. 'Churchwardens accounts' in THOMPSON, K. M. ed. *Short guides to records, Second series, guides 25-48.* Historical Association, 1997, 11-15.

- BOTELHO, L., ed. *Churchwardens accounts of Cratfield, 1640-1660.* Suffolk Record Society **42**. 1999.
- HANHAM, ALISON, ed. *Churchwardens accounts of Ashburton, 1479-1580.* Devon & Cornwall Record Society New series **15**. 1970.
- BAILEY, F. A., ed. *The churchwardens' accounts of Prescot, Lancashire, 1523-1607.* Lancashire & Cheshire Record Society **104**. 1953.

Churchwardens' Presentments

The maintainance of order was one of the tasks of the churchwarden. They played a pivotal role in the ecclesiastical attempt to control morals and beliefs; their major weapon was the presentment made at the Visitation of Bishop or Archdeacon. The churchwardens were required to present everyone who offended against ecclesiastical law; such offences included matters as diverse as adultery, nonconformity, refusal to pay church rates, and non-residence of the rector, *etc.* Presentments are to be found with the records of church courts.

Citations, Bibliographic

Always cite your source! Whenever you identify relevant information in your ancestral research, make a note of where you found it, in a way that will enable you to check it again if you need to. In the case of archival material, note the relevant *record office, and any reference numbers you had to cite to call for the document. A brief description of the document, e.g. Ambridge Poor Law Accounts 1800-1850 will also be helpful.

In the case of books, citations should be in the form you would expect to find them in a library catalogue. The name of the author, and the title should be taken from the title page (rather than the cover, if there is a choice). To this should be added any edition statement (e.g. 2nd edition) the place of publication, the name of the publisher, and the date

Citations, Bibliographic (*continued*)

of publication, together with the page no(s) referred to. This page, for example, should be cited as follows:

- RAYMOND, STUART A. *The Family Historian's Pocket Dictionary.* Bury: F.F.H.S., 2003, p.58.

Civil Registration

Civil registration of births, marriages and deaths in England and Wales commenced on 1st July 1837. The country was divided into 619 registration districts (increased to 623 in 1851), each with a superintendant registrar. The superintendant maintained his own records, but also sent quarterly returns to the Registrar General. Local registrars have indexes to births, deaths and civil marriages in their districts; usually, however, they did not index marriages which took place in church. Their returns to the Registrar General were copied into the latter's registers; seperate indexes of birth, marriages and deaths were compiled each quarter. These indexes are open to public inspection; however, the registers themselves cannot be consulted. In order to obtain information from them, a certificate must be ordered.

The General Register Office indexes are now held by the Family Records Centre (previously they were at St. Catherine's House). Copies are also held by many *libraries, *county record offices, *family history societies, *etc.* Certificates may be applied for in person at the Family Records Centre, or by post from the General Register Office, P.O.Box 2, Southport, Merseyside, PR8 2JY. They may also be obtained from local registrars for events in their districts.

The information included in birth certificates includes date, place of birth, name and sex, father's name (sometimes left blank if the child was illegitimate), mother's name, including her maiden name, and the signature of the informant, with her rank and address. Marriage certificates give the date and place of marriage, names, ages and 'condition' (i.e. bachelor, spinster, widow or widower) of each partner, age (although not always precisely), their 'rank or profession' and places of residence, the names and ranks or professions of their fathers, and the signatures of witnesses. Death certificates record the date and place of death, the name of the deceased, his/her sex, age (from 1866), and occupation, the cause of death, and the signature, descriptions and residence of the informant.

These certificates provide the basic information needed to start research in family history.

Web Pages:
- Civil Registration in England and Wales
  www.genuki.org.uk/big/eng/civreg/

- Registration Districts in England and Wales (1837-1930)
  www.fhsc.org.uk/genuki/reg/

- England: Civil Registration
  www.genuki.org.uk/big/eng/CivilRegistration.html

- Births, Marriages and Deaths Registration
  www.statistics.gov.uk/registration/default.asp

Further Reading:
- WOOD, TOM. *British civil registration.* 2nd ed. F.F.H.S., 2000.
- COLWELL, STELLA. *The Family Records Centre: a users guide.* 2nd ed. Public Record Office readers guide 17. 2002.
- LANGSTON, BRETT. *A handbook to the civil registration districts of England and Wales.* Langston, 2001.
- *Using birth, marriage and death records.* Pocket guides to family history. Public Record, Office, 2000.

Clandestine Marriage
See Irregular Marriage

Clergy
Church of England clergymen are normally ordained first as deacons, then as priests; records of their ordination will be found amongst *diocesan records, as will records of their

Clergy (*continued*)

institution to benefices. Since 1858, *Crockford's clerical directory* has regularly published details of Anglican clergy. Similar works were published earlier in the nineteenth century, and most dioceses publish yearbooks which also contain lists of clergy. Most Anglican churches exhibit lists of the clergy who have served them in the past. Clergymen can also be traced using *parish records, *university registers, and a wide range of other sources. The county volumes of Raymond's *British genealogical library guides*, and also his *Occupational sources for genealogists* list much published information.

Close Rolls

The Close rolls, held by the *Public Record Office, in class C54, run from 1227 until 1903. They originally recorded 'letters close', i.e. sealed orders to royal officials on a wide range of subjects. However, they soon began to be used for the enrolment of *deeds, and a variety of other documents. In the late nineteenth century, *changes of name by deed poll were enrolled on the close rolls, as were certificates of naturalization, 1844-73.

Web sites:

• Chancery and Supreme Court of Judicature: Close Rolls 1204-1903
  www.pro.gov.uk
  Search 'C54'

Further Reading:

• *Close Rolls of the reign of Henry III preserved in the Public Record Office, A.D. 1227-1231.* H.M.S.O., 1902. A further 46 vols. cover the period to 1509.

Coats of Arms

Coats of arms originated in the twelfth century as distinguishing marks for knights in armour. They soon became hereditary and a mark of social status. This necessitated regulation, responsibility for which was laid upon the heralds.

The establishment of the College of Arms followed in 1483 or 1484, and many *heraldic visitations of the counties took place in the sixteenth and seventeenth centuries.

Those who claimed the right to a coat of arms were required to prove their descent from an armigerous ancestor, and the heralds went to considerable lengths to check such claims. It is still the case that the right to bear arms is dependent on proof of descent, or, alternatively, on obtaining a grant of arms from the heralds. It is most definitely not sufficient to have the same surname as a grantee.

Further Reading:
- WOODCOCK, T., & ROBINSON, J. M. *The Oxford guide to heraldry.* Oxford University Press, 1988.

Codicil
A codicil to a *will amends it. Sometimes several codicils to the one will will be found.

Collection for Distressed Protestants in Ireland
This collection was authorized by Parliament in order to provide relief for the sufferings of protestants during the Irish rebellion of 1642. Many of the returns survive in the *Public Record Office, listing contributors; they have been little used, but may well provide useful genealogical evidence.

Further Reading:
- GIBSON, JEREMY, & DELL, ALAN. *The Protestation returns 1641-42, and other contemporary listings: collection in aid of distressed protestants in Ireland, subsidies, poll tax, assessment or grant, vow and covenant, solemn league and covenant.* F.F.H.S., 1995.

College of Arms
The College of Arms was founded in 1483 or 1484. It had - and still has - responsibility for grants of arms in England

College of Arms (*continued*)

and Wales. Its official registers list all grants since the fifteenth century. The College has an extensive archive, unfortunately not open to the public. Research can be conducted by officers of the College, i.e., the heralds.

Further Reading:
- WAGNER, A. *The records and collections of the College of Arms.* Burke's Peerage, 1952.
- CAMPBELL, LOUISE, & STEER, FRANCIS. *A catalogue of manuscripts in the College of Arms collections. Volume 1.* College of Arms, 1988.

Web Page:
- College of Arms
  www.college-of-arms.gov.uk

Common Pleas

See Court of Common Pleas

Common Recovery

Common recovery, like the final concord (see *Feet of fines), was a collusive legal action for the purpose of property conveyance, which could take place in manorial courts, in the *Court of Common Pleas, and in various other courts. Records from the Court of Common Pleas, 1583-1834, are in the *Public Record Office, class CP43.

Commonwealth War Graves Commission

The Commission's prime responsibility is the maintainance of war graves, cemeteries and memorials of the two world wars; it also maintains the Debt of Honour Register, which is searchable on the web, and which provides a brief record of all the fallen and the location of their graves.

Web Page:
- C.W.G.C.: Commonwealth War Graves Commission
  www.cwgc.org/

Commutation

See Tithes

Company Records
See Business records

Computers
Computers are now to be found in a majority of British homes, and most readers of this book will already be familiar with features such as word processing, databases, *etc.* A variety of database programs are available, aimed specifically at genealogists, which enable you to enter details of particular individuals in your family, and map the links between them. The *Internet is now a major source of information for genealogists, and *e-mail provides a valuable means of communication with other researchers. Many books of interest to genealogists are now available on *CD. The *Society of Genealogists publishes *Computers in genealogy* every quarter; this is a good source of information on new developments.

Web Pages:
- Genealogy & Technology Articles by Mark Howells
  www.oz.net/~markhow/writing/

- Computers in Genealogy
  www.sog.org.uk/cig/
  Web-page of the journal

Further Reading:
- HAWGOOD, DAVID. *Using computers for genealogy.* An introduction to ... series, 2nd ed. F.F.H.S., 1998.

Confirmation
See Baptism

Congregationalists
The Congregationalist churches (otherwise known as Independents) insist on the right of each congregation to govern itself. As is the case with most other *nonconformist denominations, their registers of baptisms, marriages and deaths pre-1837 are mostly in the *Public Record Office,

Congregationalists (*continued*)

classes RG4 and RG8. Other records may be found at Dr. Williams Library, and in *county record offices. Clifford provide a list.

Further Reading:

- CLIFFORD, DAVID J. H. *My ancestors were Congregationalists in England and Wales. How can I find out more about them?* Rev. ed. Society of Genealogists, 1997.
- 'The three denominations: the Presbyterians (including Unitarians) Independents (or Congregationalists) and Baptists', in STEEL, D. J. *Sources for nonconformist genealogy and family history.* National index of parish registers 2. Society of Genealogists, 1973, 519-600.

Conservation

Family historians need to be aware of the dangers that threaten books, papers and other records - including, increasingly, computers. Archivists and librarians are very aware of the way in which paper, for example, can deteriorate, and of the need for adequate environmental conditions in which to store their materials.

Family historians too need some basic knowledge. Not only do they need to understand how unique materials should be handled in the archives - pencils, not pens, no folding of pages, no leaning on manuscripts, no direct tracing - but they also need an appreciation of how to care for the documents that they themselves compile, or which they have inherited. Acid-free paper, for instance, is essential when compiling documents intended for posterity - you don't want it all to flake away in fifty years time. You should avoid exposing documents and photographs to too much light - especially direct sunlight: it will cause them to fade. All photographs should be stored in acid-free photo-albums, which are frequently advertised in genealogical magazines. Sellotape should never be used: it disintegrates remarkable quickly and ruins any documents to which it may be attached.

Web Page:
- Cyndis List: Preservation and Conservation
  www.cyndislist.com/preservation.htm
- Advice on Caring for your Books and Documents at Home
  **www.norfolk.gov.uk/council/departments/nro/
  nrocons.htm**

Further Reading:
- BAYNES-COPE, A. D. *Care of books and documents.* British
  Museum Publications, 1981.

Constables

The constable was originally a manorial officer, but the
decay of the manor led parochial vestries to begin making
the appointment during the 17th and 18th centuries. He was
responsible for collecting taxes, maintaining law and order,
and raising the local *militia; he was usually appointed on a
rotation basis from the more substantial members of the
community. Where constables' *accounts have survived they
can be useful to the genealogist. His activities can also be
traced in the records of *Quarter Sessions.

Further Reading:
- KENT, JOAN. *The English village constable, 1580-1642: a
  social and administrative study.* Clarendon Press, 1986.
- BENNETT, MARTIN. Constables accounts' in THOMPSON, K.
  M., ed. *Short guides to records. Second series, 25-48.*
  Historical Association, 1997, 16-20.
- FOX, LEVI, ed. *Coventry constables' presentments 1629-
  1742.* Publications of the Dugdale Society **34**. 1986.

Conveyance

See Title Deeds

Convicts and Prisoners

Many people have unwillingly fallen (and continue to fall)
into the hands of the law, and the possibility that an
ancestor was imprisoned should not be ignored by

Convicts and Prisoners (*continued*)

researchers. Criminal records are extensive, and may also reveal information about witnesses, policemen and lawyers.

The administration of justice was the responsibility of *Assizes and *Quarter Sessions, and their records contain much information of value; they are to be found in the *Public Record Office and *county record offices respectively. Their responsibility for prisons was transferred to the Home Office in 1877, and hence many prison records are in the Public Record Office.

The more serious cases were referred to the *assize courts, whose judges had commissions of *gaol delivery. Criminal cases might also be heard in the *Court of Kings Bench and a variety of other courts.

Until the end of the eighteenth century, prisons were used primarily for the custody of those awaiting trial, the correction of vagrants, and the coercion of debtors (see *Bankruptcy and Insolvent Debtors). Most convicted felons were either executed or transported. Transportation to North America ceased in 1776, and convicts were confined to hulks moored in the Thames, at Portsmouth and at Plymouth, until the convict colony of New South Wales was founded in 1788. The sentence of transportation was abolished in 1887. All gaoled offenders were known as prisoners; those sentenced to transportation were convicts.

Web Page:

- Sources for Convicts and Prisoners 1100-1986
  catalogue.pro.gov.uk/Leaflets/ri2195.htm

Further Reading:

- HAWKINGS, DAVID T. *Criminal ancestors: a guide to historical criminal records in England and Wales.* Sutton Publishing, 1992.
- SCALE, MICHELLE. *Law and society: an introduction to sources for criminal and legal history from 1800.* Public Record Office readers guide 14. 1996.

- PALEY, R. *Using Criminal Records.* Public Record Office, 2001.
- LAMOINE, GEORGES, ed. *Bristol gaol delivery fiats 1741-1799.* Bristol Record Society **40.** 1989.

Copyhold

Under this form of tenure, land was held by virtue of a copy of an entry in a manorial court roll (see *manors). The services due to the manorial lord in the medieval period were commuted into monetary payments in the early modern period, and leasehold tenure tended to replace copyhold in the same period. However, copyhold was not finally abolished until 1925.

Copyright

Copyright in both published and unpublished material (including web pages) is owned by authors, or by whoever has purchased the right to them. It lasts for the life-time of the author, and for 70 years from his or her death - or 70 years from the date of publication if published posthumously. Works must not be copied without the permission of the author or copyright owner, although brief quotations for the purpose of criticism or review are permissible. Copyright includes both published and unpublished material, and even extends to the words spoken by interviewees on tape (they own the copyright). This means that copyright may exist in archival sources: if you want to publish them, you must check whether you need permission with the relevant *record office.

Web Page:
- What is Copyright Protection?
  www.whatiscopyright.org

- Copyright
  www.pro.gov.uk/about/copyright/copyright.pdf

Coroners

Coroners were first appointed in 1194 to investigate the causes of unnatural, suspicious and sudden deaths. That continues to be their prime funtion today, although they have had other duties e.g. dealing with treasure trove. For the genealogist, their records contain valuable information on the circumstances and causes of death.

Further Reading:

* GIBSON, JEREMY. *Coroners records in England and Wales.* 2nd ed. F.F.H.S., 1997.
* COLE, JEAN A., & ROGERS, COLIN D. 'Coroners inquest records', in THOMPSON, K. M., ed *Short guides to records. Second series, guides 25-48.* Historical Association, 1997, 114-7.
* HUNNISETT, R. F., ed. *Sussex coroners inquests 1485-1558.* Sussex Record Society **74**. 1985.

Counties

The English counties are the primary administrative areas for English local government; their pre-1974 boundaries mostly date from Anglo-Saxon times (the northern counties were formed a little later, and there were also a few minor changes in the course of the last millenium). The Welsh counties were created by the Act of Union in 1536. After 1888, sub-divisions of Yorkshire (the 3 ridings), Lincolnshire (the 3 parts), Suffolk (East and West), and Sussex (East and West) acted as independent counties, as did the Isle of Ely, the Soke of Peterborough, and the Isle of Wight.

The naming of English counties is sometimes problematic for Americans. With one exception - County Durham - the word 'county' is not a part of the name of any county in the way that it is in Ireland. Many, however, do have the suffix '-shire' as the last part of the name; in some cases, e.g. Devon or Devonshire, this is optional.

For genealogists, the importance of counties is that many of the original sources needed for research were either created by county administrative organs (such as *quarter sessions) or are filed or indexed by county (e.g. *hearth tax records). It is always important to know which county a place is in, or which county a family came from.

Web Page:
- British Counties, Parishes, etc., for Genealogists
  homepages.nildram.co.uk/~jimella/counties.htm

Country
In the nineteenth century and earlier, a word used to refer to a person's home county or, more loosely, neighbourhood.

County Families
County families are the members of the elite in each county, both *gentry and *aristocracy. Their pedigrees are usually to be found in the returns of sixteenth and seventeenth century *heraldic visitations and in the nineteenth and twentieth century collections of publishers such as Burke's. Many *biographical dictionaries are also available; reference should be made to the listing in section 7 of RAYMOND, S. A. *English genealogy: a bibliography.* 3rd ed., F.F.H.S., 1996.

Further Reading:
- *Burke's family index.* Burke's Peerage, 1976.

County Histories
County histories of the nineteenth and early twentieth centuries are often invaluable sources of genealogical information - especially those which survey the histories of each individual parish. These often contain pedigrees, manorial descents, monumental inscriptions, extracts from parish registers and other original sources, *etc., etc.* The *Victoria County History* (V.C.H.) is the most well known example of the genre. The county volumes of Raymond's *British genealogical library guides* identify the most useful histories for each county.

Further Reading:
- CURRIE, C. R. J., & LEWIS, C. P. *English county histories: a guide.* Stroud: Alan Sutton, 1994.

County Record Offices

The rapid expansion of county record offices in the second half of the twentieth century helped fuel the explosion of interest in genealogy, by ensuring that the archival sources genealogists need to consult are easily available (although that is not their prime function). The records of *Quarter Sessions are their core holdings, but many now also serve as diocesan record offices. Most also hold *parish records, as well as the archives of a variety of private estates, businesses and semi-public bodies.

It is advisable to be well prepared when visiting county record offices. Before you visit, check out their web sites or hand-books. Consult the county bibliographies in Raymond's *British genealogical library guides* to find out what material from the archives has already been published and can be consulted in *libraries. Be aware of the difference between the county record office and the *local studies library, and preferably visit the latter first: *books there will probably tell you what parish registers are available in the record office, and may also lead you to other archival sources. The entry for *record offices provides further information, including details of where you can find addresses.

Court Baron

The court baron was the manorial court concerned with copyhold land, the custom of the manor, and the services due to the lord. See *Manor.

Court Leet

The court leet dealt with law and order and the administration of communal agriculture. See *Manor.

Court of Arches

The Court of Arches was the Archbishop of Canterbury's provincial court of appeal. It dealt primarily with *Prerogative Court of Canterbury probate business, but also with matrimonial, moral, tithe and other ecclesiastical matters. Its records survive from the 16th century and have been published on microform. See:

- *Records of the Court of Arches 1554-1911: Lambeth Palace Library.* Microform. Chadwyck-Healey, c.1983. Indexed in: HOUSTON, J. *Index of cases in the records of the Court of Arches at Lambeth Palace Library 1660-1912.* Index Library **85.** British Record Society, 1972.

Court of Augmentations

In the 16th century, Henry VIII augmented the revenues of the Crown by dissolving the monasteries and seizing their property. The Court of Augmentations was established in 1535 to administer the lands and revenues which were about to fall into the hands of the crown. The court was amalgamated with the *Court of Exchequer in 1554; its records are in classes E315 and E321 in the *Public Record Office.

Further Reading:

- NICHOLLS, YVONNE. *Court of Augmentations accounts for Bedfordshire.* 2 vols. Publications of the Bedfordshire Historical Record Society **63-4.** 1984-5.
- YOUINGS, JOYCE, ed. *Devon monastic lands: calendar of particulars for grants, 1536-1558.* Devon & Cornwall Record Society, New series **1.** 1955.

Court of Chancery

The office of Chancellor dates from the eleventh century, when he was the leading minister of the Crown. The earliest surviving records of his 'Court of Chancery' begin in 1199, and the long-running series of *Close Rolls, *Patent Rolls and Charter Rolls, all contain valuable information for the

Court of Chancery (*continued*)

genealogist. Chancery began to operate as a court of law from 1348. It was a court of equity, concerned with disputes between individuals, especially concerning land. Its records survive in profusion at the *Public Record Office, and are exceptionally rich in information for the family historian. They fall into three main categories: proceedings, registers, and exhibits. This, however, is a fairly simplistic division: there are no less than 63 separate classes of Chancery equity records in the Public Record Office - and there is no comprehensive index. The *Bernau index at the Society of Genealogists may help to provide a way in; Horwitz provides the essential guide, and lists various finding aids.

Web Pages:

- Chancery Masters and Other Exhibits: Sources for Social and Economic History
  catalogue.pro.gov.uk/Leaflets/ri2259.htm

- Chancery Proceedings: Equity Suits from 1558
  catalogue.pro.gov.uk/Leaflets/ri2240.htm

- Chancery: Masters Reports and Certificates
  catalogue.pro.gov.uk/Leaflets/ri2257.htm

- The Equity Pleadings Database
  www.pro.gov.uk/equity/

Further Reading:

- HORWITZ, HENRY. *Chancery equity records and proceedings: 1600-1800.* 2nd ed., Public Record Office handbook **27**. 1993.
- GERHOLD, DORIAN. *Courts of equity: a guide to Chancery and other legal records.* Pinhorn Handbook **10**. 1994.
- HORWITZ, HENRY, & MORETON, CHARLES. *Samples of Chancery pleadings and suits: 1627, 1685, 1735 and 1785.* List and Index Society **257**. 1995.

Court of Common Pleas

This court had common law jurisdiction in civil cases. Its records of property disputes include many fictitious actions intended to provide a formal record of title to land (see *Feet of Fines and *Common Recovery).

Further Reading:

- HASTINGS, MARGARET. *The Court of Common Pleas in fifteenth century England: a study of legal administration and procedure.* Ithaca: Cornell University Press, 1947.

Court of Exchequer

From the mid-sixteenth-century, the Court of Exchequer developed an equity jurisdiction, hearing many disputes concerning land title, manorial rights, tithes, debts, wills, *etc.* This business was transferred to the Court of Chancery in 1841. Its records include pleadings, depositions, affidavits, surveys, exhibits, and decrees and order books, and sometimes provide much detail. The *Bernau index indexes the Exchequer depositions in E134; other finding aids are listed in:

- Equity Proceedings in the Court of Exchequer **catalogue.pro.gov.uk/Leaflets/ri2237.htm**

Further Reading:

- HORWITZ, HENRY. *Exchequer equity records and proceedings 1649-1841.* Public Record Office Handbook **32**. 2001.
- HORWITZ, HENRY, ed. *London and Middlesex Exchequer Equity pleadings, 1685-6 and 1784-5: a calendar.* London Record Society **35**. 1998.

Court of Great Sessions

This court was established in 1542, and functioned until 1830. It exercised similar jurisdiction in the Principality of Wales to that exercised by *assizes in England. Its records are in the *National Library of Wales. They include plea rolls, *feet of fines, gaol files, *etc., etc.* These records are

Court of Great Sessions (*continued*)

voluminous, and capable of yielding much valuable information, but may be difficult to use.

Web Page:

- Records of the Court of Great Sessions
  www.llgc.org.uk/lc/lcs0040.htm

Further Reading

- PARRY, GLYN. *A guide to the records of the Court of the Great Sessions.* National Library of Wales, 1995.
- CHAPMAN, MURRAY Ll. 'The records of the Court of Great Sessions for Wales', in ROWLANDS, JOHN, & ROWLANDS, SHEILA, eds. *Welsh family history: a guide to research.* 2nd ed. F.F.H.S., 1998, pp.191-209.

Court of Kings Bench

Kings Bench was the highest court of common law in the realm, and exercised jurisdiction in both civil and criminal actions. Its records are extensive; probably the most useful for the family historian are the depositions of witnesses.

Web Page:

- Kings Bench (Crown Side) 1675-1875
  catalogue.pro.gov.uk/Leaflets/ri2252.htm

Court of Requests

This court was established in 1483; its records cease in 1642. It was intended to provide simple procedures for poor men to bring civil writs, although, as is the way of the world, it attracted much business from court circles. It dealt with matters such as title to property, annuities, villeinage, wilful escape, forgery, marriage contracts, etc.

Web Pages:

- Court of Requests 1485-1642: a court for the poor
  www.pro.gov.uk/leaflets/ri2222.htm

Further Reading:

- LEADAM, I. S., ed. *Select cases in the Court of Requests A.D. 1497-1569.* Publications of the Selden Society **12**. 1898.

Court of Star Chamber

This court was revived by Henry VIII but because associated with mis-use of the royal prerogative under the early Stuarts, and was abolished by Parliament in 1641. It had, originally, been popular because it provided quick redress cheaply. Its surviving records are in English, are mostly well indexed, and the depositions in particular often reveal intimate personal information.

Web Page:

- The Court of Star Chamber Court 1485-1642
  www.pro.gov.uk/leaflets/ri2221.htm

Further Reading:

- GUY, J. *The Court of Star Chamber and its records to the reign of Elizabeth I.* Public Record Office handbooks **21.** H.M.S.O., 1985.
- *List of the Proceedings in the Court of Star Chamber preserved in the Public Record Office. Vol. 1. A.D. 1485-1558.* Lists and indexes **13.** Reprinted Kraus Reprint, 1963. Indexed in Lists and indexes supplementary series **4.**
- *Proceedings in the Court of Star Chamber vol. 2[-5]. Elizabeth I.* Lists and indexes supplementary series 4(2-5). Kraus Reprint, *et al,* 1969-75.
- BARNES, T. G., ed. *List and index to the proceedings in Star Chamber for the reign of James I (1603-1625) in the Public Record Office, London, class STAC8.* 3 vols. Chicago: 1975.
- LEADAM, I. S., ed. *Select cases before the King's council in the Star Chamber, commonly called the Court of Star Chamber.* 2 vols. Selden Society **16** & **25.** 1903-11. Covers 1477-1544.

Court of Wards and Liveries

Lands held of the King in chief were subject to wardship if they fell by inheritance into the hands of a minor. The King was entitled to the profits of the estate during the minority;

Court of Wards and Liveries (*continued*)

he had the right to choose the ward's marriage partner, and to enter his inheritance. In practice, the King usually sold these rights to the highest bidder. The Court of Wards and Liveries was established in the early 1540's, to take over the administration of wardship from the *Court of Chancery.

The records of the Court (WARD 1-15) include *inquisitions post mortem,* usually copied from the original, which was filed with the records of the *Court of Chancery, the feodary's certificates of the values of each estate, and the purchasers 'confession' of its value which included notes on encumbrances such as debts, legacies, jointures *etc.*. There are also pleadings, depositions, deeds, extents, *etc.*. These are invaluable sources if your ancestors were landowners.

Web Page:
• Court of Wards and Liveries 1540-1645: Land Inheritances
  www.pro.gov.uk/leaflets/ri2229.htm

Further Reading:
• BELL, H. E. *An introduction to the history and records of the Court of Wards and Liveries.* Cambridge University Press, 1953.
• HURSTFIELD, JOEL. *The Queens wards: wardship and marriage under Elizabeth I.* Longmans, Green & Co., 1958.
• HAWKINS, M. J., ed. *Sales of wards in Somerset 1603-1641.* Somerset Record Society **67.** 1965.

Court Rolls

Court rolls record the proceedings of manorial courts, and are vital sources of genealogical information where parish registers are not available. They begin in the 13th century, and a few continued until 1925. Unfortunately, they are in *Latin until the mid-18th century. Their importance is due to the fact that they record the inheritance of copyhold land from father to son. Quite a number have been published by *record societies, and are listed in *Texts and calendars;*

indeed, one record series - the *Wakefield Court Rolls* series, published by the Yorkshire Archaeological Society - is exclusively devoted to the rolls in one very extensive manorial archive. See also *Manors.

Further Reading:
- HARVEY, P. D. A., ed. *Manorial records of Cuxham, Oxfordshire, circa 1200-1359.* Oxfordshire Record Society, 50., 1976.

Courts Martial

Offences against army discipline are tried by courts martial, as are offences against ordinary law committed by a member of the armed forces. There were various different types of court martial, but virtually all surviving records of army courts are from the office of the Judge Advocate General, now in the *Public Record Office. Its registers, 1796-1963, give name, rank, regiment, place of trial, charge, binding and sentence for each case tried. There are also reports submitted to the relevant authority for confirmation of the sentences, and other miscellaneous proceedings and papers.

Web Pages:
- British Army: Courts Martial, 17-20th centuries
  catalogue.pro.gov.uk/Leaflets/ri2022.htm

  British Army: Courts Martial: First World War, 1914-1918
  catalogue.pro.gov.uk/Leaflets/ri2295.htm

Further Reading:
- ORAM, GERARD. *Death sentences passed by the military courts of the British Army, 1914-1924,* ed. Julian Putkowski. Francis Boutle Publishers, 1998.
- PUTKOWSKI, J. *British Army mutineers, 1914-1922.* Francis Boutle Publishers, 1998.

Cousin German

First cousin

Crime and Criminals
See Convicts and Prisoners

Crockfords
Crockfords directory, first published in 1858, lists Church of England clergy who currently hold appointments or have recently retired.

Curate
This term was often used of any clergy serving a parish church, but since the seventeenth century has usually only applied to an assistant priest paid a salary, and removable by the incumbent or bishop. Curates had normally to be licensed by the bishop, and licensing records are to be found amongst *diocesan records.

Curia Regis
The Curia Regis was the Kings court, from which developed the Courts of Kings Bench, Exchequer, and Common Pleas. Its rolls provide much information on disputes between landowners, *etc.*

Further Reading:
- *Curia regis rolls ... preserved in the Public Record Office.* 18 vols. H.M.S.O., *et al,* 1922-99. Covers 1189-1245. More vols. forthcoming.

D

Dates

In the course of research, the genealogist is likely to come across various methods of dating, and in particular, needs to be aware of the alteration from the Julian to the Gregorian calendar in 1752, when England 'lost' eleven days, due to the discrepancy between the two calendars:

2nd September 1752 was followed by 14th September. At the same time the old custom of commencing the official year on 25th March was abandoned, and 1st January became the first day of the year.

This had long been recognised unofficially, and it was conventional to write dates between 1st January and 25th March as 1688/9. This is still good practice for family historians.

Documents - and especially official documents - may also be dated by the regnal year; this is still the practice with acts of parliament; 51 Elizabeth II runs from 6th February 2002. Manorial records frequently date by saints days. If you are using legal records, you may also come across references to the law terms - Michaelmas (late September to end November), Hilary (mid-January to mid-February), Easter from Easter to April or May), and Trinity (mid-May to 24th June).

Web Pages:

- Chronology and Dating
  www.genealogy.medieval.org.uk/guide/chron.shtml

Further Reading:

- CHENEY, C. R. *A handbook of dates for students of British history.* New ed. Royal Historical Society guides and handbooks **4**. Cambridge University Press, 2001.

- WEBB, CLIFFORD. *Dates and calendars for the genealogist.* Society of Genealogists, 1994.

Daughter-in-law

Daughters-in-law were often referred to as daughters in old records. Conversely, step-daughters may be referred to as daughters-in-law.

Death

The event of death has been recorded in various ways down through the centuries, and a variety of records are available for the family historian. There are articles in this book on *Inquisitions post mortem* *parish registers, *probate records, *monumental inscriptions, personal announcements in *newspapers, *death duty registers, *obituaries, *nonconformist registers, and *civil registration.

Death Certificates

See Civil Registration

Death Duty Registers

Death duties were first imposed in 1796, and were based on the value of estates. The death duty registers at the *Public Record Office provide a great deal of information on the deceased, including name, last address and occupation, details of executors, and of the distribution of the estate. They may include much information on the family of the deceased, and usually indicate where the will was proved. Indexes are in class IR27, and registers in IR26. Some are on microfiche; others may require 3 days notice for production.

Web page:
- Death Duty records from 1796
  catalogue.pro.gov.uk/Leaflets/ri2164.htm

Decree

The judgement or sentence of a court.

Deed Poll

A deed usually involving only one person, and hence 'polled' i.e. cut smooth, rather than indented (see *indenture). Deed polls are most commonly used for *changes of name.

Deeds

See Title Deeds, Leasehold Tenure, Lease and Release

Deeds Registries

Deeds registries for each of the three Ridings of Yorkshire, and for Middlesex, were established in the early eighteenth century. A similar registry for the Bedford Levels was established in 1663 and functioned until 1920. Registration was voluntary, but millions of deeds were registered, since registration made it easier to prove title to land. No genealogist tracing families in the areas covered by these institutions should neglect them.

Web Pages:
* The Middlesex Deeds Registry 1709-1938
  **www.cityoflondon.gov.uk/leisure_heritage/
  libraries_archives_museums_galleries/lma/pdf/
  middlesex_deeds.PDF**

* The East Riding Register of Deeds: a guide for users
  **www.eastriding.gov.uk/learning/archives/pdf/
  deedsnet.pdf**

Further Reading:
* SHEPPARD, F., & BELCHER, V. 'The deeds registries of Yorkshire and Middlesex', *Journal of the Society of Archivists* 6(5), 1980, 274-86.

Deforciant

A person who wrongfully ejects or keeps another out of the possession of an estate. The term is sometimes found in legal records.

Demography

Demography is the study of population. The study of English historical demography relies greatly on two sources that are also of prime interest for the genealogist, i.e. *parish registers and the *census. Co-operation between genealogists and demographers benefit both. Wrigley and Schofield's *Population history* is not easily read, but it is a magisterial example of what can be done by co-operation between everyone interested in parish registers. See also *CAMPOP.

Further Reading:
- WRIGLEY, E. A., & SCHOFIELD, R. S., *et al. The population history of England, 1541-1871: a reconstruction.* Edward Arnold, 1981.

Denization

Grants of denization conferred some of the rights of Crown subjects upon aliens, but not full naturalization. In particular, denizens were able to own land, but not to inherit it, nor could they hold offices of trust or receive grants of crown land. Denization was conferred by letters patent, which can be found enrolled in the patent rolls, c.1400-1844 (Classes C66 and C67 in the Public Record Office). See also *Immigrants and aliens

Further Reading:
- PAGE, WILLIAM. ed. *Letters of denization and acts of naturalization for aliens in England, 1509-1603.* Publications of the Huguenot Society **8**. 1893. Continued for 1603-1700 in v.18, and for 1701-1800 in v.27, with a supplement in v.35.

Deponent

A witness who makes a deposition under oath.

Depositions

Depositions are statements made under oath in a court of law. In the sixteenth and seventeenth centuries it was usual for deponents to make oral or written statements, frequently in response to interrogatories. These depositions frequently contain information likely to be of use to the family historian, and may usually be found with the records of particular courts.

Dewey Decimal Classification

Most public libraries use the Dewey classification scheme to arrange their books on the shelves. It is worth remembering that genealogy is at 929, and English history is at 942. The bibliography of genealogy, however, is at 016.929. Particular subjects may be sub-divided by place; for example, 929.0942 is English genealogy.

Dexter

The right hand side of a coat of arms, viewed from the back.

Diaries

If you are lucky enough to find a diary of one of your ancestors, then you may have access to his private thoughts, or at least to details of his day to day activities. Diaries may provide details of the comings and goings of relatives and friends, and may even provide dates and places of births, marriages and deaths. Even if you cannot find diaries compiled by your own family, you should not neglect to check those of other people in the locality, which may refer to your family. Many diaries have been published; many more may be found in record offices.

Further Reading:

- MATTHEWS, W. *British diaries: an annotated bibliography of British diaries written between 1642 and 1942.* Berkeley: University of California Press, 1950.
- HAVLICE, P. P. *And so to bed: a bibliography of diaries published in English.* Metuchen, N. J.: Scarecrow Press, 1987.

Diaries (*continued*)
- MACFARLANE, ALAN. *The diary of Ralph Josselin, 1616-1683.* Records of social and economic history. New series **3**. Oxford University Press for the British Academy, 1976.
- SPALDING, RUTH, ed. *The diary of Bulstrode Whitelocke 1605-1675.* Records of social and economic history. New series **13**. Oxford University Press for the British Academy, 1990.
- BAGLEY, J. J., ED. *The great diurnal of Nicholas Blundell of Little Crosby, Lancashire.* 3 vols. Record Society of Lancashire and Cheshire **110, 112, & 114.** [1968-72.]

Dictionary of National Biography
The *D.N.B.,* as it is commonly referred to, is the major British biographical dictionary. It provides brief biographies of people who have been eminent in British life from the earliest times to 1900; decennial supplements since then include those who have died in the decade covered. A new edition is currently in preparation. Copies of the *D. N. B.* are usually available in public libraries. A new edition is in preparation; details are given on the web page.

Web Page:
- New Dictionary of National Biography
  www.oup.co.uk/newdnb/

Dimunitives
See Nicknames

Diocese
A diocese is the area over which a bishop exercises ecclesiastical authority. Prior to the reformation (mid-sixteenth century) there were seventeen dioceses in England, and four in Wales. A further six were created by Henry VIII following the dissolution of the monasteries, taking territory from some of the excessively large medieval dioceses. In the nineteenth and twentieth centuries, a further twenty have been founded.

Anglican dioceses should not be confused with those of the Roman Catholics, which were re-established in England following the restoration of the Roman hierarchy in 1850.

Diocesan Records

Diocesan records include *bishops registers, *act books, records of the church courts, *bishops transcripts, visitation records, *estate records, licences for curates, schoolmasters, surgeons, preachers, and non-conformist meeting houses, *probate records, ordination registers and papers, and a wide variety of other letters and papers. They can be found in diocesan record offices, which are usually amalgamated with *county record offices.

Directories

See Trade Directories

Distraint of Knighthood

Any gentleman with lands worth over £40 per annum was considered worthy of knighthood. Charles I sought to raise money by levying a fine - a distraint - on those who had failed to take up knighthood at his coronation. Assessments of c.1629 to 1635 are in the *Public Record Office, class E178/7154; a full list is at class E407/35.

Distressed Protestants in Ireland

See Collection for Distressed Protestants in Ireland

Divorce

Prior to 1858, the only way to obtain a divorce in England and Wales was by act of Parliament - a remedy which was very expensive and only open to the wealthy. Separation was, however, an option; this could be achieved by private agreement, desertion, wife sale (!) or judicial separation by the church courts.

The Matrimonial Causes Act 1857 transferred the responsibility for marital disputes to the civil courts.

Divorce files from 1858 to 1943 are in the Public Record Office at class J77 (indexes in J78). Later records are still held by the Principal Registry of the Family Division, First Avenue House, 42-49, High Holborn, London, WC1V 6NP.

Web Pages:
- Divorce Records before 1858
  catalogue.pro.gov.uk/Leaflets/ri2288.htm

- Divorce Records after 1858
  catalogue.pro.gov.uk/Leaflets/ri2289.htm

Domesday Book

Domesday book is the earliest systematic survey of land ownership in England (although it excludes some northern counties, London, and Winchester). It was initiated by William the Conqueror in 1086, to discover who held what and how much each manor was worth. For the genealogist, it provides a comprehensive list of manorial lords, and a base-line beyond which it is extremely unlikely that ancestors could be traced. If you find an ancestor in domesday book you are doing well (and can hardly be considered to be a beginner!)

The original manuscript is in the *Public Record Office. However, full transcripts are readily available: the Phillimore edition provides one or two volumes for each county, and is also available on CD. Many transcripts for particular counties are also available in the *Victoria county history*, and in various other publications.

Web Site:
- Domesday Book
  catalogue.pro.gov.uk/Leaflets/ri2108.htm

Further Reading:
- MORGAN, PHILIP. *Domesday book and the local historian.* Help for students of history **95.** Historical Association, 1988.

Dormant Peerage

A dormant peerage is a peerage for which no heir can be traced.

Dr. Barnardo's

See Barnardo Homes

Dr. Williams Library

This library, founded under the will of a Presbyterian minister, is a theological library which has extensive collections on the history of nonconformity.

In addition to its book collection, it maintained a register of non-conformist baptisms from 1742 to 1837 (now in the *Public Record Office, RG4/4658-65, with indexes at RG4/4666-76.) It still has a card index of Congregationalist ministers, and a variety of other manuscripts, many of them likely to be of use to family historians.

E

Easter Book

Easter books, found with *parish records, record the dues
that were paid to the incumbent by Church of England
communicants at Easter - normally no more than a shilling.
They are effectively lists of heads of households, and as such
invaluable sources for both genealogists and demographers.

Further Reading:
- WRIGHT, S. J. 'A guide to Easter books and related parish
  listings', *Local population studies* **42**, 1988, 18-31; **43**, 1989,
  13-27.

East India Company

The British colonisation of India largely took place under the
auspices of the East India Company, which was founded in
1600, and taken over by the crown after the Indian Mutiny of
1857. Service in the Company was regarded as a high-road to
fortune, and many middling families sent their children to
the company's college at Haileybury, and thence to India, as
Company servants. The extensive records are now in the
British Library's *Oriental and India Office Collections.

Ecclesiastical Courts

See Church Courts

Ecclesiastical Visitations

In theory, bishops were supposed to 'visit' their dioceses
every three years; archdeacons their archdeaconries every
year. A visitation involved summoning ministers and
*churchwardens, *etc.,* to attend, and issuing visitation
articles indicating the subjects to be investigated - which

would include topics such as church fabric, attendance at church, the living, charities, non-conformity, *etc.* The clergy and churchwardens would compile replies responding to each question asked in the articles, and report on the conduct of parishioners since the previous visitations. Once their presentments had been made, the bishop or archdeacon, would determine the need for any action, and have injunctions issued by his registrar. See also *church courts.

Further Reading:

- OWEN, DOROTHY M. 'Episcopal visitations books', in MUNBY, L. M., ed. *Short guides to records. First series, guides 1-24.* Historical Association, 1994, 49-53.
- BRINKWORTH, E. R. C., ed. *Episcopal visitation book for the Archdeaconry of Buckingham, 1662.* Buckinghamshire Record Society 7. 1947.
- COOK, MICHAEL, ed. *The Diocese of Exeter in 1821: Bishop Carey's replies to queries before visitation.* 2 vols. Devon & Cornwall Record Society, N.S., 3 & 4. 1958-60.
- KITCHING, C. J., ed. *The royal visitation of 1559: act book for the Northern Province.* Surtees Society 187. 1975.
- RANSOME, MARY, ed. *Wiltshire returns to the Bishop's Visitation Queries 1783.* Wiltshire Record Society 27. 1972.

Educational Records

See *School records and *University Registers

Electoral Registers

Electoral registers record the names of those entitled to vote at Parliamentary and local government elections. Electoral registration began in 1832, and registers have been issued annually since then, except in 1917 and from 1940 to 1944. Their coverage has extended as the franchise has been widened; since 1928 they have included the names and addresses of all adults who have registered.

Survival of electoral registers is patchy. The British

Electoral Registers (*continued*)

Library holds a good collection, and registers for the local area ought to be available in local studies libraries and county record offices. With the exception of the British Library collection, surviving registers are listed by Gibson and Rogers.

Web Page:
- United Kingdom Electoral Registers and their uses
  www.bl.uk/services/information/spis_er.html

Further Reading:
- GIBSON, JEREMY, & ROGERS, COLIN. *Electoral registers since 1832; and burgess rolls.* 2nd ed. F.F.H.S., 1990.

E-mail

E-mail provides an invaluable means of making contact with other genealogists, and with libraries and record offices. A variety of mailing lists, newsgroups, message / query boards, surname *interests lists, *etc.,* are available on the *internet enabling you to identify and exchange information with those who have similar interests to yourself.

Web Pages:
- Genealogy Resources on the Internet: United Kingdom Mailing Lists
  **www.rootsweb.com/~jfuller/
  gen_mail_country_unk.html**

- F.A.Q: Mailing Lists: What are they for?
  helpdesk.rootsweb.com/help/maill.html

Emigration and Emigrants

Emigration has always been a feature of British history; we know, for example, that many Anglo-Saxons fled to Byzantium after the Norman Conquest. Large-scale movements since then have, however, been dependent upon English colonial developments.

The plantation of Ulster in the sixteenth century saw the first important movement, followed by the colonisation of

North America and the West Indies. Many went as indentured servants; many more suffered transportation. Emigration did not cease with American independence; poverty, politics and enterprise continued to persuade many to head for North America throughout the nineteenth century and into the twentieth.

Transportation of convicts to the *United States did, however, cease at independence; consequently, it was re-directed to *Australia, which soon became a destination (with *New Zealand) for free settlers as well. Meanwhile, the *East India Company was developing its trade with *India, and many went there as company servants - although most intended to return when they had made their fortune. The East India Company also opened up the possibility of emigration to *South Africa when the British occupied the Cape to secure the route to India in 1806. The thirst for gold subsequently opened up the Transvaal to settlement, as it had already opened up California and south-eastern Australia.

Sources for tracing emigrants are numerous, both in England and in the emigrants' new countries. *Passenger lists and *passport records are both obviously relevant; less obvious are the records of *poor law overseers, who may have assisted paupers to emigrate and thus relieve the burden on the rates. Many servants seeking a better life entered into indentures to serve for a number of years in exchange for a passage, board, and payment in cash or land at the end of their service; many indentures are held at the *Public Record Office and *Guildhall Library. Many children were sent overseas by philanthropic organizations; some are recorded in the *Child Migrant Index. A wide variety of other records are available, especially in the Public Record Office, and in the archives of each colony. Reference should also be made to entries for particular countries.

Web Page:
- Emigrants
  catalogue.pro.gov.uk/Leaflets/ri2272.htm

Further Reading:
• KERSHAW, ROGER. *Emigrants and expats: a guide to sources on UK emigration and residents overseas.* Public Record Office readers guide, **20**. 2002.

Enclosure Awards

Between 1700 and 1900 about 7,000,000 acres of land was enclosed from what had previously been open fields. Apart from the dramatic change in the landscape, the process of enclosure produced extensive documentation, including detailed lists of landowners and tenants in enclosure agreements and awards.

In the seventeenth century, these can often be found amongst the records of Chancery and other courts; subsequently, enclosure was frequently effected by private Act of Parliament. The General Inclosure Act 1836 rendered private acts unnecessary. Copies of enclosure awards were made for parish records, and for the clerk of the peace; they may now be found in county record offices, although some are held by the Public Record Office.

Web site:
• Enclosure Awards
www.pro.gov.uk/leaflets/ri2193.htm

Further Reading:
• TATE, W. E. 'Enclosure awards and acts' in MUNBY, L. M., ed. *Short guides to records. First series 1-24.* [Rev. ed.]. Historical Association, 1994, 77-8
• TATE, W. E. *A domesday of English enclosure acts and awards.* Reading: University of Reading Library, 1978.
• SANDELL, R. E. *Abstracts of Wiltshire inclosure awards and agreements.* Wiltshire Record Society **25**. 1971.

Entail

Entails enabled landowners to ensure that family land remained in the hands of the family, and prevented heirs from alienating it. Entailment meant that each heir had a life interest only; he could not sell the freehold, as he had no permanent interest in it. Leases of entailed land reverted to the heir on the lessors death. Entailed land was said to be held in fee tail. Entails ceased to be effective in 1833.

Entry Fines
Tenants were usually required to pay an entry fine on entering their property; such fines are recorded in manorial *court rolls, in leases (see *leasehold), and in various other *estate records.

Epitaphs
See Monumental Inscriptions

Equity
In the medieval period, the king was the fount of justice. He was frequently petitioned to 'do justice' where the common law could not provide a remedy to aggrieved subjects. Consequently, a number of courts evolved to meet the demand for equity, that is, judgement by conscience or justice, rather than the common law. These included the Court of Chancery, the Court of Exchequer, the Court of Star Chamber and the Court of Requests.

Escheat and Escheators
When a tenant died without an heir, his land was said to escheat to his lord. Escheators were the officials who ensured that land held of the king escheated to him; on the death of a tenant in chief they called together a jury to hold an *inquisition post mortem*.

Esquire
Esquires were originally knights' shield-bearers. By the sixteenth-century they became men entitled to a *coat of arms, and superior to the ordinary *gentry. In the nineteenth century the term began to be used in addressing letters to gentlemen, and later to all men.

Essoin

An essoin was effectively an apology for non-attendance at a manorial court, entered at the beginning of court rolls with a note of the fine imposed for absence.

Estate Duty Records

See Death Duty Records

Estate Records

The majority of houses in England are now owner-occupied. It was not always so. In medieval times and later most of England was divided up into manors, which often - although not always - covered entire parishes. Most manors were owned by a single lord. Many manorial lords owned more than one manor, and some landed estates were very extensive.

The administration of even the smaller estates necessarily generated a mass of paper - *accounts, *title deeds, leases (see *Leasehold), *rentals, *surveys, correspondence, *maps, *etc.* These records contain masses of information likely to be of interest to family historians. Find out the name(s) of the landowners in the places where your ancestors lived; they can easily be found in *county histories. Then see if you can trace their *archives. They may be in the local *county record office - but not necessarily. Estate archives moved with families and have been widely dispersed; most county record offices have records from other counties, and the major national repositories - the *British Library, the *Public Record Office *etc.* - also have extensive collections; indeed, some collections are now overseas. The *National Register of Archives is able to advise on locations; however, its published listing only identifies 120 of the most extensive collections.

Further Reading:

- *Principal family and estate collections.* 2 vols. Guides to sources for British history based on the National Register of Archives 10-11. H.M.S.O., 1995-8.

- FOX, H. S. A., ed. *The Cornish lands of the Arundells of Lanherne, fourteenth to sixteenth centuries.* Devon & Cornwall Record Society. New series **41**. 2000.
- PHILLIPS, C. B., ed. *Lowther family estate books 1617-1675.* Surtees Society **191**. 1979.
- SMITH, A. HASSELL, BAKER, GILLIAN M., & KENNY, R. W., eds. *The papers of Nathaniel Bacon of Stiffkey.* 3 vols. Norfolk Record Society **46, 49,** & **53.** 1979-88.

Exchequer

See Court of Exchequer

Extent

An extent is a detailed survey of a manor or estate, listing tenants, and showing the rents and services due to the lord.

Extents for Debt

Extents for debt describe and value the lands and goods of defaulting debtors. They are kept in the Public Record Office, in C131 and C239.

Further Reading:

- CONYERS, ANGELA. ed. *Wiltshire extents for debts, Edward I - Elizabeth I.* Wiltshire Record Society **28.** 1973.

Extra-Parochial District

The division of England into parishes was haphazard, and left behind some districts which were not part of any parish. Such areas were exempt from levies such as church and poor rates, and sometimes tithes. Baptisms, *etc.,* would be conducted at whatever church was most covenient. All extra-parochial districts became civil parishes in 1894.

F

Faculty Office
The Faculty Office of the Archbishop of Canterbury shared with the Vicar General the task of issuing marriage licences on behalf of the Archbishop.

Family
Historically, this term encompassed a wider range of people than it does today: it included all members of a household, including servants, apprentices, *etc.* In genealogical usage, the term usually refers to all those of the same surname descended by the male line from a single ancestor.

Family Bible
In the nineteenth-century, family bibles often included pages for the entry of family births/baptisms, marriages and deaths. These bibles have often been handed down in families, and it is always worth asking relatives if they know of the existence of such a volume.

Web Page:
• British Family Bibles
  www.familybibles.co.uk

Family Division
See Principal Registry of the Family Division

Family Histories and Pedigrees
Many family histories and pedigrees have been published; many more are to be found in manuscript in local studies libraries and record offices. It is always worth asking such institutions whether they have any material relating to your family. Published material is much easier to track down, since usually at least several institutions hold the same

book. There are also numerous articles in genealogical and historical journals which are widely available in *libraries. An attempt to list all of them is being made in Raymond's *British genealogical library guides* series. Articles in family history society journals are indexed in *Family history news and digest.* Most pedigrees published prior to 1975 are listed in one of the following title:

- MARSHALL, G. W. *The genealogists guide.* 4th ed. Heraldry Today, 1967. Originally published 1903. For pedigrees published pre-1903.
- WHITMORE, J. B. *A genealogical guide: an index to British pedigrees in continuation of Marshall's genealogists guide.* Walford, 1953. Also published as Harleian Society **90, 101, 102 & 104.** For pedigrees published 1904-50.
- BARROW, G. B. *The genealogists guide: an index to printed British pedigrees and family histories 1950-1975.* Research Publishing, 1977.

Reference may also be made to:

- THOMSON, T. R. *A catalogue of British family histories.* 3rd ed. Research Publishing Co., for the Society of Genealogists, 1976:
- McCOLVIN, L. R. *The Librarian's subject guide to books. Vol. 2. Biography, family history, genealogy, etc.* James Clarke & Co., 1960.

Many family history web pages are also available, some with considerable detail; they are usually being up-dated regularly with new information. To find them, visit:

- A-Z of Family Surnames from England
  members.tripod.com/~Caryl_Williams/names-7.html

- Personal Homes Pages
  www.cyndisList.com/personal.htm

- Websites at Rootsweb: Surname Resources
  www.rootsweb.com/~websites/surnames/

Family History

The object of the family historian is to understand his ancestors in their historical context, and to seek an appreciation of the way in which they lived their lives. This goes far beyond the genealogical task of assembling the bare bones of pedigrees from birth/baptism, marriage and death/burial records. Family historians are seeking their 'roots': those roots cannot be seen simply by drawing a pedigree chart. Consequently, it is desirable to develop an awareness of the historical background, both local and national, and also an understanding of the diversity of sources that may throw light on family history. See also *genealogy

Family History Centers

Family History Centers are branches of the *Church of Jesus Christ of Latter Day Saints' Family History Library in Salt Lake City. They are able to borrow most of the millions of microfilm and fiche in that library, and hold its catalogue on fiche. Most Centers also have on-line access to *Family Search, and small collections of books, CD's *etc.* There are numerous Centers in the United Kingdom, listed on the web.

Web Pages:

- What is a Family History Center?
  **www.familysearch.org/Eng/Library/FHC/
  library__fhc__about.asp**

- Family History Centres
  www.lds.org.uk/genealogy/fhc/index.htm
  List of UK Centers

- LDS Information
  www.genuki.org.uk/big/LDS/
  Addresses with notes on the catalogue

Family History Library

See Church of Jesus Christ of Latter Day Saints

Family History News & Digest

This magazine is the 6 monthly journal of the *Federation of Family History Societies. It includes news of current events, reports of the activities of member societies, authoritative book reviews, and a digest section listing articles *etc.* published in the journals and newsletters of local societies. It also has an up-to-date listing of all member societies. It is available from F.F.H.S. (Publications) Ltd., Units 15-16, Chesham Industrial Centre, Oram St., Bury, BL9 6EN.

Family History Societies

There are now over 150 family history societies in the United Kingdom, most of which are members of the Federation of Family History Societies, (see *Family History news and digest* for up to date listings). The majority of societies are county based; however, there are also many specialist societies devoted, for example, to Anglo-German genealogy or cemeteries in South Asia. There are also many one-name societies, most of which are members of the *Guild of One Name Studies (Goons). The *Society of Genealogists is both the oldest established, and the largest society.

Most societies have regular meeting programmes and publish a journal; the latter usually includes members interest lists, in addition to news, and brief articles (abstracted in *Family history news and digest.*)

Many societies are also engaged in transcribing and (sometimes) publishing sources such as *parish registers and *monumental inscriptions. Some have extensive publishing programmes in booklet or fiche forms; a few are now also publishing on CD. Most have their own libraries, some of which are extensive, e.g. Berkshire Family History Society is making a determined effort to collect all family history society journals published in England. A directory of family history society resources is planned by the present author.

- Family History Societies
www.genuki.org.uk/Societies/
Links to society web-pages.

- Federation of Family History Societies: List of Member Societies
www.ffhs.org.uk/General/Members/index.htm

Family Reconstitution
Family reconstitution is a technique used by historical demographers, and especially by *CAMPOP, to measure demographic change in particular places. It is based on *parish registers, which are analysed in depth to 'reconstitute' the families of the parish.

Family Records Centre
The Family Records Centre, 1, Myddleton Street, London, EC1R 1UW, is jointly run by the General Register Office and the Public Record Office. It houses the records of *civil registration, together with *census and *probate records, and some *non-conformist registers.

Web Page:
- Family Records Centre
www.familyrecords.gov.uk/frc.htm

Further Reading:
- COLWELL, STELLA. *The Family Records Centre: a users guide.* 2nd ed. Public Record Office readers guide 17. 2002.
- COLLINS, AUDREY. *Using the Family Records Centre.* Basic facts about ... series. F.F.H.S., 1997.

Family Search
This is the genealogical website of the *Church of Jesus Christ of Latter Day Saints, offering access to a variety of resources, including the *International genealogical index, *Ancestral file, the Family History Library catalogue, *etc.*

- Family Search
  www.familysearch.org

- How to use Family Search
  www.pro.gov.uk/research/leaflets/fsearch.htm

Family Tree
See Pedigree

Family Tree Magazine
This is the leading English family history journal, published commercially once a month. It includes many articles, book reviews, a computer section, readers interests, and news updates; it campaigns on matters of genealogical interest such as access to the Registrar General's records. Its sister publication, aimed at beginners, is *Practical Family History.* It is published by ABM Publishing Ltd., 61, Great Whyte, Ramsey, Huntingdon, Cambs., PE26 1HJ.

Web Page:
- ABM Publishing Ltd.
  www.family-tree.co.uk

Farmer
It was only in the eighteenth century that this term began to be used of a person who rents and cultivates a farm. It has now entirely superseded the earlier 'yeoman', which in its turn replaced the medieval 'franklin'. Originally, a farmer was a person who purchased the right to collect taxes for a fixed sum; if he collected more, he made a profit:

Father in Law
A term that was often used to refer to step-fathers.

Fealty
The feudal system required every new tenant to take an oath of allegiance to the king, at the same time as he paid homage to his lord. This was termed 'fealty'.

Federation of Family History Societies

The Federation is a UK based organisation which represents, advises, and supports, over 220 member societies world-wide. It was founded in 1974, and sponsors half-yearly conferences hosted by different member societies each time. Its journal, *Family History news and digest,* includes regular reports on its activities. Major projects have included indexing the 1881 census, (in conjunction with the Genealogical Society of Utah), the *British Isles Genealogical Register* (BigR) and the *National Burials Index.* A variety of other projects are on-going.

The Federation's publishing programme is also extensive. Major series have included the *Gibson guides* to particular sources, the *British genealogical library guides* series, the beginners *Introduction to …* series, and Raymond's *F.F.H.S. web directories.* Many other individual titles have also been published, such as the present book.

Web Page:
- Federation of Family History Societies
  www.ffhs.org.uk

Fee Simple

A freehold estate, free of all dues to the lord, and disposable at will by the tenant.

Fee Tail

See Entail

Feet of Fines

Fines, or final concords, were a means of officially recording the transfer of land. They were the end result of a fictitious dispute in the Court of Common Pleas between a *querunt* - the grantee - and the deforciant - the grantor. The text of the final concord was copied on to a single parchment, which was cut into three portions along indented lines (the indents were intended to prevent forgery if the portions were brought together again). One portion was given to each party; the third portion, i.e. the foot (hence 'feet of fines', or *pedes finium*) was retained in the Court's archives. They survive from the 1180's until 1833 in the *Public Record Office. Fines may also be frequently found amongst estate records.

Many fines have been published, both nationally and for specific counties; details are given in *Texts and Calendars*, in the county volumes of Raymond's *British genealogical library guides*, and also on the web pages listed below. Older publications are likely to be in *Latin.

Fines are not necessarily easy to interpret, and ought to be studied in conjunction with other title deeds. The real nature of the transaction may not be apparent from the fine itself. Nevertheless, the mere mention of names in them is good genealogical evidence. The books cited below contain useful introductions to this source.

Web Pages:
- Public Records: Feet of Fines
  www.medievalgenealogy.org.uk/guide/fin.shtml

- Land Conveyances: Feet of Fines 1182-1833
  catalogue.pro.gov.uk/Leaflets/ri2220.htm

Further Reading:
- FOSTER, C. W., ed. *Final concords of the County of Lincoln from the feet of fines preserved in the Public Record Office A.D. 1244-1272, with additions from various sources, A.D.1176-1250.* Lincoln Record Society **17**. 1920.
- DODWELL, BARBARA, ed. *Feet of fines for the County of Norfolk for the tenth year of the reign of King Richard the First, 1198-1199, and for the first four years of the reign of King John, 1199-1202.* Pipe Roll Society. New series **27**. 1950.

Fencibles
Fencibles were regular regiments liable for home service only; they are often classed with the *Militia. Some muster books

are in the *Public Record Office, class WO13; other records may be found in county record offices.

Web Page:
- Fencible Regiments of the British Army 1793-1814
  www.regiments.org/milhist/uk/lists/fen1793

Feodary
This term has several inter-related meanings. It may signify a survey of the obligations of crown tenants, the official who enforces those obligations, or a person who holds such obligations.

Feoffment
The most ancient form of land conveyance known to archivists is the feoffment. The actual transfer of property took place through the ceremony of *livery of seizin. The feoffment merely confirmed the seizin. Such feoffments normally commence with the words *Sciant presentes ...,* i.e. 'know all men ...'

Feudalism
This term is often used to describe Norman society, although it had its counterpart in other European societies. All land was held of the king in return for military service. The barons granted their manors to retainers for knight service; manorial lords demanded various services from their peasants. The system began to break down in the thirteenth and fourteenth centuries, as the various services due were commuted into monetary payments.

Fiche
See Microfiche

Final Concords
See Feet of Fines

Finding Aids

Every record office has finding aids to help you to identify the particular documents you need. These may be simple lists of documents, or full calendars giving detailed abstracts. Some of these finding aids will include indexes as well. You need to know what finding aids are available for each class of record likely to be of interest to you.

Fines

In previous centuries, a fine was not necessarily a penalty for infringing the law, although it could be that. It might equally be a method of conveyancing or a payment made to the crown, or a lord, for the grant of an office or some other privilege. See also *feet of fines, *fine rolls, and *entry fines.

Fine Rolls

The fine rolls in the Public Record Office (C60) take their name from the enrolment on them of fines, i.e. payments made for writs, grants, licences, *etc.* They also include many documents issued under the Great Seal relating to matters in which the crown had a direct financial interest. Hence they include many grants of office, orders to royal officials, grants of wardship and marriage, writs for the *livery of seizin, *etc.* The medieval fine rolls have been published.

Further Reading:
- *Calendar of the fine rolls preserved in the Public Record Office.* 22 vols. H.M.S.O., 1911-62. Covers 1272-1509.

Fire Insurance Records

Fire insurance companies were first established in London in the late seventeenth-century and in the provinces in the eighteenth century. Policy registers contain much information of interest to family historians; they are likely to record the name, status, occupations, and address of the policyholder, details of the property insured, and names of

Fire Insurance Records (*continued*)

any tenants. Records of over 80 companies are held at the Guildhall Library; Cockerell & Green also list many records deposited in county record offices and elsewhere.

Web Page:

- Fire Insurance Records at Guildhall Library
  www.ihrinfo.ac.uk/gh/fire.htm

Further Reading:

- THOMAS, J. H. 'Fire insurance policy registers', in MUNBY, L. M., ed. *Short guides to records. First series, 1-24.* [Rev.ed.] Historical Association, 1994, 97-100.
- COCKERELL, H.A.L., & GREEN, EDWIN. *The British insurance business: a guide to its history and records.* 2nd ed. Sheffield Academic Pres, 1994.
- CHAPMAN, STANLEY D., ed. *The Devon cloth industry in the eighteenth century: Sun Fire Office inventories of merchants' and manufacturers' property, 1726-1770.* Devon and Cornwall Record Society, New Series **23**. 1978.

Fleet Prison

A prison for debtors. Many irregular marriages took place there.

Forfeited Estates Commission

This Commission was established in order to administer the estates forfeited by Jacobite rebels following the rebellion of 1715. Its archives include many estate records, especially from northern England; its rentals and surveys are particularly likely to be of interest to genealogists.

Further Reading:

- BARLOW, D. *The records of the Forfeited Estates Commission.* Public Record Office handbooks **12**. H.M.S.O., 1968.

Foundlings

Foundlings were abandoned babies, who became the responsibility of the parish. There is frequent mention of foundlings in *parish registers, *poor law records, *constables accounts, *etc.* In London, Captain Coram opened his Foundling Hospital in 1745; thousands of children passed through its doors.

Further Reading:

- McCLURE, RUTH K. *Coram's children: the London Foundling Hospital in the eighteenth century.* New Haven: Yale University Press, 1981.

Franchise

The franchise is the right to vote. Historically, the qualification for voting has varied considerably, especially in borough constituencies. Prior to the 1832 Reform Act, the borough franchise depended on the borough charter, and sometimes its custom. There could be as few as 12 voters in a borough, although in a few boroughs - especially Westminster - the franchise was very wide, and thousands voted. In the counties, by contrast, the franchise was accorded to all those who owned freehold property worth over forty shillings per annum.

The Reform Act of 1832 widened the franchise considerably, although it was still based on property. It was widened still further in 1867, 1884 and 1918, but it was not until 1928 that there was full adult suffrage; a further extension took place in 1969 when those aged between 18 and 21 were granted the franchise.

The importance of the franchise to family historians is that, until 1832, the names of voters were recorded in *poll books. Since then, all those eligible to vote have been listed in *electoral registers. These sources are invaluable for tracing the distribution of particular surnames over wide areas.

Frankpledge

The system of frankpledge imposed corporate responsibility on groups of ten or twelve men, to ensure that offenders against the law were brought to justice. If one member of the frankpledge (or tithing) offended, the whole frankpledge could be fined if the offender failed to appear in court. The manorial 'view of frankpledge' was held regularly to ensure that everyone was a member of the frankpledge.

Freebench

Freebench was the right of widows to hold a part or all of their husbands copyhold land, subject to the custom of the *manor.

Freehold

Freehold land was originally land not held by a servile tenure, not subject to manorial custom, and perhaps held by knight service or in socage. Freeholders enjoyed the security of tenure in perpetuity; if they owned lands worth over forty shillings per annum, their names may be found in lists of *jurors, and in *poll books.

Freeholder Lists

See Jurors

Freemasons

The origins of freemasonry are obscure, but its recorded history in England dates from the seventeenth century. Lodges were originally independent, but in 1717 began to recognise the authority of a national grand lodge. If an ancestor is thought to have been a freemason, you should read:

- LEWIS, PAT. *My ancestor was a freemason.* Society of Genealogists, 1999.

Freemen

Most medieval boroughs were governed by freemen, who had various rights and privileges, dependent on the borough charter(s) and on custom. These rights usually included exclusive rights to vote, and to conduct a trade, in the borough. They ceased in 1835.

Freemen were usually members of a city guild or livery company; indeed, as in the case of London, the freedom of the city sometimes required such membership. Borough records frequently include lists of freemen, giving names, dates of admission, and sometimes trades and parentage. A number of freemens' rolls have been published.

Further Reading:
- ALDOUS, VIVIENNE E. *My ancestors were freemen of the City of London.* Society of Genealogists, 1999.
- ROWE, MARGERY M.,& JACKSON, ANDREW M. eds. *Exeter freemen 1266-1967.* Devon and Cornwall Record Society extra series 1. 1973.
- MALDEN, JOHN. *Register of York freemen, 1680 to 1986.* York: William Sessions, 1989.

French Immigrants
The French are our closest neighbours on the continent, and it is not surprising that, until the eighteenth century, they provided more immigrants to England than any other country. Most of William I's barons were from Normandy or Brittany, and movement across the Channel continued long after the Conquest. In the sixteenth century French iron workers and glassmakers brought new technology to England; they were soon followed by French Huguenots, who brought with them the word 'refugee'. More French refugees arrived during the French Revolution in the late eighteenth-century, to be followed by French prisoners of war, some of whom stayed.

Many leaflets on French research are available from the Anglo-French Family History Society. See also *immigrants and aliens.

French immigraants (*continued*)
   Web Site:
   • Anglo-French Family History Society
     anglo-french-fhs.org/

Further Reading:
   • PONTET, PATRICK. *Ancestral research in France: the
     simple guide to tracing your family history through
     French records.* Andover: Patrick Pontet, 1998.
   • PONTET, PATRICK. *Ancestral research in Paris: a guide to
     using the variable sources in family history research.*
     Andover: Patrick Pontet, 1998.

Friends
   See Society of Friends

Funerals
   Funerals are rarely discussed by genealogical authors.
   However, local newspapers in the late nineteenth and early
   twentieth centuries frequently carried detailed accounts,
   listing everyone who attended. For those of armigerous rank,
   the heralds compiled funeral certificates giving similar
   information. Some of them are in the *College of Arms
   collections; others in the *British Library. A number have
   been published. Funeral cards were popular in the Victorian
   and Edwardian era, and may have been handed down. All
   these sources provide valuable information.

Further Reading:
   • RYLANDS, JOHN PAUL, ed. *Cheshire and Lancashire funeral
     certificates, A.D.1600 to 1678.* Lancashire and Cheshire
     Record Society, **6**. 1882.
   • KING, THOMAS WILLIAM, ed. *Lancashire funeral
     certificates.* Chetham Society old series, **75**. 1869.

G

Gaol Delivery

Assize judges held commissions of gaol delivery which authorized them to try all prisoners in their circuits. The calendars of prisoners so 'delivered', compiled by sheriffs, are in the *Public Record Office, classes JUST3 and PL25.

Gavelkind

This custom of inheritance, whereby land was divided equally amongst all brothers on the death of the father, was common in Kent.

Gazetteers and Topographical Dictionaries

The importance of place in genealogical research cannot be over-emphasised, particularly place in the context of administrative areas. Archives emanate from particular administrative bodies - manors, quarter sessions, parishes, *etc.* - and the genealogist, therefore, needs to locate those bodies which are likely to have recorded the presence of his ancestors. Gazetteers and topographical dictionaries provides the means to do this. Bartholomew's is an invaluable gazetteer for locating particular - and often obscure - places. Lewis provides a brief potted history of every parish and many hamlets, indicating county, hundred, archdeaconry, *etc.*. Youngs provides a detailed listing of administrative units, including the many boundary changes.

Web Pages:

- Gazetteer of British Place Names
  www.gazetteer.co.uk

- Genuki Gazetteer
  www.genuki.org.uk/big/eng/Gazetteers.html

- Landranger
  www.ordsvy.gov.uk/products/Landranger/
  From the Ordnance Survey

Further Reading:

- BARTHOLOMEW, JOHN. *The survey gazatteer of the British Isles.* 9th ed. Edinburgh: John Bartholomew & Son, 1943. Earlier editions may also be useful.
- LEWIS, S. A. *A topographical dictionary of England ...* 4/5 vols. 7 editions. S. Lewis & Co., 1831-49.
- YOUNGS, FREDERIC A. *Guide to the local administrative units of England.* 2 vols. Royal Historical Society guides & handbooks 10 & 17. 1980-91.

Gedcom

Many family historians now run computer programs to record genealogical data. In order to transfer data between programs, it has to be in a format that both programs recognise. The Gedcom standard has been developed to facilitate such transfers.

Web Page:

- The Gedcom Standard Release 5.5
  homepages.rootsweb.com/~pmcbridge/gedcom/55gctoc.htm

- Family Search Questions: Gedcom
  www.familysearch.org/eng/Home/FAQ/faq_gedcom.asp?color=green

Genealogical Society of Utah

This institution runs the genealogical activities of the *Church of Jesus Christ of Latter Day Saints.

Web Page:

- The Genealogical Society of Utah
  www.gensocietyofutah.org/

Genealogists magazine

This is the magazine of the *Society of Genealogists, which has been published quarterly since 1925. Its articles are of general interest to all family historians; it also has many reviews of books, news, and detailed lists of accessions to the Society's library.

Genealogy

Genealogy involves the compilation of family trees from the evidence of primary sources such as *parish registers and the records of *civil registration. As such, it is a necessary preliminary to the study of *family history, which seeks an understanding of families in the historical context in which they lived.

General Register of Births, Deaths and Marriages

See Civil Registration

General Register Office

See Civil Registration

Genfair

Genfair is a web-based family history fair, with stands from over 100 organizations, including family history societies, publishers, bookshops, professional genealogists, *etc.*

Web Site:
- Genfair
  www.genfair.com

Gentlemans Magazine

This was one of the earliest monthly magazines, and is invaluable to the genealogist for its obituaries, marriage announcements and other personal announcements. It was published between 1731 and 1868; the full text of issues from 1731 to 1750 are available in the *Internet Library of Early Journals*. A typescript index of names is held by the Family

Gentlemans Magazine (*continued*)

History Library of the *Church of Jesus Christ of Latter Day Saints. Farrar's and Nangle's indexes cover briefer time-spans.

Web Site:

- Gentlemans Magazine
  oulibl.open.ac.uk/wh/resources/gentlemag-help.htm
  Covers 1731-80

Further Reading:

- CHRISTIE, P. 'The *Gentlemans magazine* as a source for the family historian', *Genealogists magazine* **20**, 1981, 238-9.
- FARRAR, R. H. *An index to the biographical and obituary notices in the Gentlemans Magazine 1731-80.* Index Library **15.** British Record Society, 1891.
- NANGLE, B. *The Gentlemans Magazine biographical and obituary notices, 1781-1819: an index.* New York: Garland, 1980.

Gentry

The gentry constituted that social class which was superior to the yeomanry, but inferior to the peerage. The heralds attempted to restrict the term to those who could claim entitlement to a coat of arms: that was the purpose of *heraldic visitations. However, the attempt failed, and in popular usage the term was gradually extended to all those who did not work with their hands. See also *county families.

Germany

Many German protestant refugees came to England in the sixteenth and seventeenth centuries. The accession of the Hanoverian dynasty attracted German businessmen in the eighteenth century; they continued to be attracted to industrial centres throughout the nineteenth century.

A variety of guides to German ancestry are available from the Anglo-German Family History Society; who also have a number of useful indexes compiled by L. Metzner. See also *immigrants and aliens.

Web Page:
- Anglo-German Family History Society of London, England **www.feefhs.org/uk/frgagfhs.html**

Further Reading:
- BAXTER, A. *In search of your German roots: a complete guide to tracing your ancestors in the Germanic areas of Europe.* 3rd ed. Baltimore: Genealogical Publishing, 1994.

Gibson Guides

The *Gibson guides* published by the F.F.H.S., provide much valuable information on sources for family and local historians. Those currently available include:

- GIBSON, JEREMY. *Bishop's transcripts and marriage licences, bonds and allegations; a guide to their location and indexes.* 5th ed. F.F.H.S., 2001.
- GIBSON, JEREMY, & CREATON, HEATHER. *Census returns 1841-1891 in microform: a directory to local holdings in Great Britain; Channel Islands; Isle of Man.* 6th ed. F.F.H.S., 1988.
- GIBSON, JEREMY, & ROGERS, COLIN. *Coroners records in England and Wales.* 2nd ed. F.F.H.S., 1997.
- GIBSON, J. S. W. *The hearth tax, other later Stuart tax lists, and the Association oath rolls.* 2nd ed. F.F.H.S., 1996.
- GIBSON, J.S.W., & MILLS, DENNIS. *Land and window tax assessments, 1690-1950.* 2nd ed. F.F.H.S., 1998.
- GIBSON, JEREMY, & CREATON, HEATHER. *Lists of Londoners.* 3rd ed. F.F.H.S., 1997.
- GIBSON, JEREMY, & MEDLYCOTT, MERVYN. *Local census listings 1522-1930: holdings in the British Isles.* 3rd ed. F.F.H.S., 2001.
- GIBSON, JEREMY, LANGSTON, BRETT, & SMITH, BRENDA W. *Local newspapers 1750-1920; England and Wales; Isle of Man: a select location list.* 2nd ed. F.F.H.S., 2002.
- GIBSON, JEREMY & HANSON, ELIZABETH. *Marriage and census indexes for family historians.* 8th ed. F.F.H.S., 2000.

Gibson Guides (*continued*)

- GIBSON, JEREMY, & MEDLYCOTT, MERVYN. *Militia lists and musters, 1757-1876.* 4th ed. F.F.H.S., 2000.
- GIBSON, J.S.W. *Poll books c.1696-1872: a directory to holdings in Great Britain.* 3rd ed. F.F.H.S., 1994.
- GIBSON, JEREMY, & ROGERS, COLIN. *Poor law union records.* 4 vols., 2nd ed. F.F.H.S., 1997-2000.
- GIBSON, JEREMY & DELL, ALAN. *The Protestation returns, 1641-42, and other contemporary listings.* F.F.H.S., 1995.
- GIBSON, JEREMY, & CHURCHILL, ELSE. *Probate jurisdictions: where to look for wills.* 5th ed. F.F.H.S, 2002.
- GIBSON, JEREMY. *Quarter sessions records for family historians: a select list.* 4th ed. F.F.H.S., 1995.
- GIBSON, JEREMY, & PESKETT, PAMELA. *Record offices: how to find them.* 9th ed. F.F.H.S., 2002.
- GIBSON, JEREMY, & HAMPSON, ELIZABETH. *Specialist indexes for family historians.* 2nd ed. F.F.H.S., 2000.
- GIBSON, JEREMY, & DELL, ALAN. *Tudor and Stuart muster rolls: directory of holdings in the British Isles.* F.F.H.S., 1989.
- GIBSON, JEREMY, & HUNTER, JUDITH. *Victuallers licences: records for family and local historians.* 2nd ed. F.F.H.S., 1997.

Glebe Terriers

Glebe terriers are records of the property and customs of particular ecclesiastical benefices. They record the glebe - the land - of the rector or vicar in detail, often referring by name to neighbouring landowners, and usually including the names of the incumbent and churchwardens. Many are held with *diocesan records for the sixteenth to eighteenth centuries. The names recorded in them may be useful evidence to family historians.

Web Page:
- Glebe Terriers
  www.le.ac.uk/elh/pot/emp/notes.html

Further Reading
- BARRATT, D.M. 'Glebe terriers', in MUNBY, L.M. ed. *Short guides to records. First series, 1-24.* Historical Association, 1994, 73-6.
- POTTS, RICHARD, ed. *A calendar of Cornish glebe terriers 1673-1735.* Devon and Cornwall Record Society. New series **19**. 1974.
- BARRATT, D.M. ed. *Ecclesiastical terriers of Warwickshire parishes.* 2 vols. Dugdale Society publications **22** & **27**. 1955-71.

God-parents
Godparents take responsibility for making the baptismal vows on behalf of the child(ren) they sponsor at baptism. There were normally two godparents of the child's own sex, and one of the other. Godparents frequently influenced christian names.

Goons
See Guild of One-Name Studies

Gravestones
See Monumental inscriptions

Great Britain
The name refers solely to the main island of the British Isles, which is occupied by England, Scotland and Wales.

Great Sessions
See Court of Great Sessions

Greenwich Hospital
See Royal Greenwich Hospital

Gregorian Calendar
See Dates

Gretna Green
See Border Marriages

Guardians

See Boards of Guardians

Guild of One-Name Studies

A one-name study aims to research all occurrences of the surname being studied, rather than a particular pedigree. The Goons, as they are known, acts as a clearing house for such studies. Its register lists fully constituted UK societies, UK family correspondence groups, individual specialists, and overseas groups. They also issue the *Journal of One Name Studies* and other publications, run an internet discussion group for members, and hold regular meetings. All researchers should check their register.

Web Page:

* Guild of One Name Studies
  www.one-name.org/intro.html

Guildhall Library

Guildhall Library, Aldermanbury, London, EC2, specialises in the history of London, but also has extensive collections of biographical and genealogical books and journals for the whole country. Its collections of pollbooks and trade directories, for example, are amongst the best in the country; there are also many published parish registers, genealogical microfiche, and local histories, as well as numerous county and family history society journals.

Its archival collections primarily relate to the City of London - parish records, livery company archives, business records, *etc.* However, it is not responsible for the archives of the Corporation of London. It also holds many registers of baptism, marriages and burials from British churches overseas, deposited by the Bishop of London, together with unpublished indexes and transcripts of various genealogical sources.

Web Pages:
- Guildhall Library
  **www.cityoflondon.gov.uk/leisure__heritage__/
  libraries__archives__museums__galleries/
  city__london__libraries/guildhall__lib.htm**
- Guildhall Library Manuscripts Section
  ihr.sas.ac.uk/gh/

Further Reading
- HARVEY, RICHARD. *A guide to genealogical sources in
  Guildhall Library.* 4th ed. Guildhall Library, 1997.

Gypsies

Gypsies are not easy to trace, although not impossible.
There are many references to them to be found in parish and
Quarter Sessions records. The Romany and Traveller Family
History Society specialises in gypsy research.

Web Sites:
- Romany & Traveller Family History Society
  website.lineone.net/~rtfhs

- Gypsy Collections at the University of Liverpool
  sca.lib.liv.ac.uk/collections/gypsy/intro.htm

Further Reading:
- FLOATE, SHARON SHILLERS. *My ancestors were gypsies.*
  Society of Genealogists, 1999.

H

Hand-Writing

Palaeography is the study of old hand-writing. Prior to the
eighteenth century, styles of hand-writing were very
different from the modern norm, and practise in reading
them is needed.

Documents in English such as *parish registers and *wills
can usually be read, but persistence may be necessary. It is
often a matter of knowing what to expect, and of comparing
difficult letters with those used elsewhere in the document.
*Latin documents are more difficult, due not only to the
unfamiliarity of the language, but also to the heavy use of
abbreviations, and the fact that many scribes were not good
Latinists themselves - frequently their grammar is poor.

Web Page:
- Medieval Palaeography: an introductory course
  orb.rhodes.edu/textbooks/palindex.html

Further Reading:
- BUCK, W.S.B. *Examples of English handwriting 1550-1650.*
  Phillimore for the Society of Genealogists, 1965.
- HECTOR, L.C. *The handwriting of English documents.* 2nd
  ed. Dorking: Kohler & Coombes, 1980.
- MUNBY, LIONEL. *Reading Tudor and Stuart handwriting.*
  Phillimore for the British Association for Local History,
  1988.

Hardwicke's Act
See Marriage Act 1753

Harleian Society
The Harleian Society, founded in 1869, is best known for the
many volumes of *heraldic visitations of the English

counties it has published. Its *parish register publications
are also important, especially for London. These books are
fully listed in *Texts and calendars*. Full details of the
Society can be had from its secretary at the College of Arms,
Queen Victoria Street, London, EC4V 8BT.

Hatchments

Diamond-shaped hatchments, painted on wood or canvas,
provide a display of the arms and heraldic insignia of the
person commemorated. Details of over 4,500 hatchments are
given in:
- SUMMERS, P., *et al*, eds. *Hatchments in Britain.* 10 vols.
  Chichester: Phillimore, 1974-94.

Hearth Tax

The hearth tax was introduced in 1662 as part of the
attempt to provide the Restoration government with a secure
regular income. It continued until 1689; however, surviving
assessments survive primarily for 1662-6 and 1669-74. The
tax was based on the number of hearths, with exemption for
houses worth under twenty shillings per annum, and for
those too poor to pay church and poor rates.

Surviving assessments are in the *Public Record Office
class E179. These are duplicates of the original assessments;
originals may occasionally be found in *county record offices.
They are usually arranged by county, hundred (or
wapentake) and parish, and list the names of all tax payers,
with the number of hearths assessed. Many have been
published by *record societies; these are listed by Gibson.
The *British Record Society has recently commenced a
project to publish all unpublished returns.

Hearth tax returns are invaluable sources for family
historians, especially when they have been published, since
they enable one to see the distribution of particular
surnames across whole counties, and thus suggest where to
look for further information.

Web Page:
- The Hearth Tax 1662-1688
  catalogue.pro.gov.uk/Leaflets/ri2139.htm

Further Reading:
- GIBSON, J.S.W. *The hearth tax, other late Stuart tax lists, and the Association Oath rolls.* 2nd ed. F.F.H.S., 1996.
- HOWELL, ROGER. 'Heath tax returns', in MUNBY, L.M., ed. *Short guides to records. First series, guides 1-24.* Historical Association, 1994. pp.45-8.
- SCHURER, KEVIN, & ARKELL, TOM, eds. *Surveying the people: the interpretation and use of document sources for the study of population in the later seventeenth century.* Oxford: Leopards Head Press, 1992.
- EVANS, NESTA, ed. *Cambridgeshire hearth tax returns, Michaelmas 1664.* Index library, **115.** British Record Society, 2000.
- SEAMAN, PETER, ed. *Norfolk hearth tax exemption certificates 1670-1674: Norwich, Great Yarmouth, King's Lynn and Thetford.* Norfolk Record Society, **65.** 2001. Also published by the British Record Society as Hearth tax series, **3.**
- WEBSTER, W.F., ed. *Nottinghamshire hearth tax 1664, 1674.* Thoroton Society record series **37.** 1988.

Heirs
See Inheritance

Heraldic Visitations

We live in an egalitarian society. Our ancestors, however, were obsessed with social status. The desire to maintain the status structure of society, and to prevent persons not entitled to armorial bearings from using them, led the heralds to institute visitations of the counties in order to verify that only those with entitlement were using coats of arms. They examined the evidence of family muniments and traditions, personal knowledge, and the records of previous visitations, in order to confirm or disallow claims. The result of their work was a huge collection of *pedigrees, now housed at the *College of Arms.

Many visitation pedigrees have been published by the *Harleian Society and other record societies (see *Texts and calendars* for details). These volumes are extremely useful; however, four caveats must be made. Firstly, the work of the heralds themselves was not necessarily accurate. Secondly, many of the published visitations are taken from copies of the original returns, and not from the originals themselves, hence introducing further possibilities of error. Thirdly, some published volumes described as 'visitation returns' actually include a great deal more information than was in the original returns, and do not necessarily make this clear. Fourthly, some works described as 'visitations' actually have nothing to do with the heralds at all, and are simply collections of pedigrees. The researcher should always check what he sees in print!

Further Reading:
- HUMPHERY-SMITH, CECIL R. *Armigerous ancestry: a catalogue of sources for the study of the visitations of the heralds in the 17th and 17th centuries.* Canterbury: Family History Books, 1997.
- SQUIBB, G.D. *Visitation Pedigrees and the genealogist.* 2nd ed. Pinhorn, 1978.
- BARNES, R. 'Heralds visitations' in JOHNSON, K.A. & SAINTY, M.R., eds. *Genealogical research directory: national and international.* 14th ed. 1994, 13-24.
- SIDDONS, MICHAEL POWELL, ed. *The visitation of Herefordshire 1634.* Publications of the Harleian Society, New series **15**. 2002.

Heraldry
If your ancestors were armigerous, i.e., entitled to a coat of arms, then a knowledge of the principles of heraldry may be useful. The fact that arms are hereditary in character, and

Heraldry (*continued*)

do not belong to everyone who has the same surname, means that their use by an ancestor can help you identify links in your pedigree - assuming that their use was legitimate. *Coats of arms do reveal links between families; an armigerous marriage enables the husband to impale his wife's shield on the sinister i.e. left-handed side of his own shield; if she is an heiress, her arms can be placed on a small shield in the centre of his own as an escutcheon. The descendants of an heiress are entitled to quarter her arms with their own; if there are several such heiresses amongst ones ancestors, then there is an entitlement to the appropriate number of 'quarters'. The rules of marshalling arms are fairly detailed and should be studied by those with armigerous ancestors. They - and indeed, all aspects of heraldry - are supervised by the heralds of the *College of Arms.

Web Pages:

- British Heraldry
  www.heraldic.org/topics/britain

- The British Heraldic Archive
  www.kwtelecom.com/heraldry

Further Reading:

- FRIAR, STEPEHN. *A new dictionary of heraldry.* Alphabooks, 1987.

- FRIAR, STEPHEN. *Heraldry for the local historian and genealogist.* Stroud: Alan Sutton, 1992.

- WOODCOCK, THOMAS, & ROBINSON, JOHN MARTIN. *The Oxford guide to heraldry.* Oxford University Press, 1996.

Heralds

See College of Arms

Heriot

The heriot was the payment due to a manorial lord on the death of a tenant. It frequently took the form of the tenant's best beast.

Historical Manuscripts Commission

This body is the British government's central advisory body on archives and manuscripts relating to British history, and the principal official source of information on them. Those aspects of its operation of particular interest to family historians include the *National Register of Archives, the Manorial Documents Register (see *Manors), and Archon (see *county record offices). It also produces many publications, in particular, its *reports and calendars* series provides extensive calendars of archive and manuscript collections. These are listed on its web site, in *Texts and calendars,* and in the county volumes of Raymond's *British genealogical library guides.*

The Commision was merged with the *Public Record Office to form a new National Archives body on 1st April 2003.

Web Site:

- Historical Manuscripts Commission
  www.hmc.gov.uk

Homage

Feudal tenure required the tenant to pay homage to his lord, i.e. take an oath of allegiance. Manorial juries were often referred to as 'the homage'.

Honour

An honour, under the Norman and Angevin kings, was a large estate centred on castles, which included many manors.

House History

Many of the sources that family historians use to trace the histories of families, may also be used to trace histories of houses. Whilst the house historian also needs an understanding of architecture - methods of construction, the various phases of building, the design - when he is in the record office, he will be reliant on *title deeds, *court rolls and other records of *manors, *taxation records, *probate

House History (*continued*)

records, rate books, *maps, *etc., etc.* The documentary sources are as relevant to the family historian as to the house historian. The two come together when the attempt is made to trace the descent of a particular property. Many such descents have been traced; county histories of the nineteenth century are full of them, as are the transactions of county historical and archaeological societies. Many articles in the latter are listed in Raymond's *British genealogical library guides.*

Web Page:
- House History
  www.hmc.gov.uk/focus/text/housesourcestxt.htm

Further Reading:
- BARRATT, NICK. *Tracing the history of your house.* Public Record Office, 2001.

House of Correction

Houses of correction were established by Quarter Sessions in the early modern period to house those convicted of offences. Inmates had to work.

House of Lords Record Office

The House of Lords Record Office holds the archives of Parliament, which mainly relate to proceedings in Parliament; few are of genealogical relevance, apart from the *Protestation returns of 1641/2, some returns of papists, papers related to private bill procedures *etc.* The address is: The Clerk of the Records, Parliamentary Archives, House of Lord's Record Office, London, SW1A 0PW.

Web Page:
- The House of Lords Record Office
  www.parliament.uk/parliamentary_publications_ and_archives/parliamentary_archives.cfm

Further Reading:
- BOND, M.F. *Guide to the records of Parliament.* H.M.S.O., 1971.

- BOND, M. *The records of Parliament: a guide for genealogists and local historians.* Canterbury: Phillimore & Co., 1964.

Household

The household was an important unit for record purposes. The heads of households were liable for imposts such as the hearth tax, and for such mundane tasks as repairing the churchyard fence; most censuses show the relationship of household members to its head. Genealogists, therefore, need a basic awareness of the structure of the household. Since medieval times, the normal household has consisted of parents, children, and perhaps, servants. Most consisted of less than five persons. Grandparents rarely lived with their grand-children: they did not live long enough. Widows and widowers frequently lived alone, although often close to their children. The extended family of popular myth has not existed in England at least since medieval times.

Huguenots

Huguenots were the first major group of refugees from religious and political persecution to find refuge in England. Many fled from France after the massacre of St. Bartholomew in 1572; more followed when Louis XVIII revoked the Edict of Nantes (which had granted them toleration) in 1685. The term is also used for Dutch Calvinists who fled the Duke of Alba's persecution in the Netherlands in 1567.

On arrival in England, many Huguenots applied for *denization or *naturalization. They also founded many churches in London and various provincial centres. Numerous records have been published by the Huguenot Society (listed in *Texts and calendars*), and the Huguenot Library holds many manuscripts and books.

Web Pages:
- The Huguenot Society of Great Britain and Ireland
  www.huguenotsociety.org.uk

- Huguenot Library
  **www.ucl.ac.uk/UCL-Info/Divisions/Library/
  huguenot.htm**

Further Reading:
- CURRER-BRIGGS, N., & GAMBIER, R. *Huguenot ancestry.*
  Phillimore, 1985.
- GRAY, IRVINE R., ed. *Huguenot manuscripts: a descriptive
  catalogue of the remaining manuscripts in the Huguenot
  Library.* Quarto series **56.** Huguenot Society, 1983.
- WELCH, EDWIN. ed. *The minute book of the French Church
  at Southampton, 1702-1939.* Southampton records series
  23. Southampton: University Press, 1979.
- GWYNN, ROBIN, ed. *Minutes of the Consistory of the
  French Church of London, Threadneedle Street, 1679-1692.*
  Quarto series **58.** Huguenot Society, 1994.

Hundred
The hundred was an administrative sub-division of a county;
its court dealt with minor offences. Many records, e.g. those
of the *land tax and the *hearth tax, are arranged by
hundred.

Husbandman
This term designated a small-holder below the rank of
yeoman, who may have had to work as a labourer as well. It
may also be used of anyone engaged in husbandry.

I

Illegitimacy

A child was illegitimate if its parents were unmarried at the time of birth. Such children are recorded in baptismal and civil registers, but the names of their fathers are usually omitted. Prior to 1750, the number of illegitimate births rarely exceeded 4% of the total.

The overseers of the poor normally endeavoured to discover the paternity of bastards. If they could, and the care of the child was likely to fall on the parish, then the father might be required to sign a bastardy bond, and to pay maintainance to the mother. Bastardy bonds are found with *parish records. Alternatively, the overseers might apply to Quarter Sessions for a maintainance order, copies of which would remain with *Quarter Sessions records. Other records of illegitimacy may be found in the records of the church courts, and in *poor law records, especially settlement examinations and overseers' accounts.

Further Reading:

- McLAUGHLIN, EVE. *Illegitimacy.* 6th ed. Haddenham: Varneys Press, 1995.
- LASLETT, PETER. OOSTERVEEN, KARLA, & SMITH, RICHARD M., eds. *Bastardy and its comparative history.* Edward Arnold, 1980.

Immigrants and Aliens

Immigration to England is not a recent phenomenon. Celts, Anglo-Saxons and Viking invaders, Norman conquerors, Huguenot refugees, Irish famine victims, persecuted East European Jews, and Jamaican bus drivers have all settled here and made their unique contribution to English society. The probability is that we all have immigrant ancestors.

Immigrants and Aliens (*continued*)

There are many records relating to immigrants. In the medieval period, discriminatory taxes were imposed on Jews and other aliens, and these records survive. Aliens who sought *denization or *naturalization left a trail of documentary evidence, much of which still survives in the *Public Record Office. During the Napoleonic wars records of aliens arriving in the country were kept. *Passenger lists contain the names of many immigrants. A wide variety of other records survive in the *Public Record Office and other record offices.

Web Page:
- Immigrants
  www.pro.gov.uk/leaflets/ri2157.htm

Further Reading:
- KERSHAW, ROGER, & PEARSALL, MARK. *Immigrants and aliens: a guide to sources on UK immigration and citizenship.* Public Record Office readers guide **22**. 2000.

Imperial War Museum

The Imperial War Museum, Lambeth Road, London SE1 6HZ has extensive collections of printed books and manuscripts relating to the history of war in the 20th century. In particular, it has an extensive collection of war diaries, letters and other personal papers likely to be of interest to family historians. There is also an extensive photographic archive.

Web Page:
- Family History Research at the Imperial War Museum
  www.iwm.org.uk/lambeth/famhist.htm

Income Tax

Income tax was first levied in 1799. It was abolished in 1802 but revived in 1803. Returns for 1799-1816, giving names of taxpayers by parish, are in the *Public Record Office, class E182. Otherwise returns rarely survive; Colley's volume is based on a unique survival.

Further Reading:
- COLLEY, ROBERT, ed. *Devizes Division income tax assessments 1842-1860.* Wiltshire Record Society **54**. 2002.

Incumbent

The incumbent is the clergyman in charge of a parish church. He may be a rector, a vicar, or a perpetual curate, and is sometimes referred to as the parson or minister (although the latter term is more frequently used of non-conformist clergy). See also *rectors and vicars.

Indenture

An indenture is a formal agreement between two parties. Two identical texts were written on one sheet, which was then 'indented', i.e. cut along a wavy line; a copy was retained by each party. If proof of the authenticity of an indenture were required at a later date, this could be checked by bringing both documents together to see if the edges matched. Indentures were used for *title deeds and a variety of other contracts, e.g. with apprentices or servants.

Indexes

Family historians rely heavily on indexes, both published, manuscript, and on the internet. An index provides a systematic list of terms in a document, collection of documents or database, and is often an essential tool for finding information, e.g. the will of a specific individual.

Indexing is frequently undertaken by volunteer family historians. It is, however, a complex task not to be undertaken lightly. Volunteer indexers should at least visit the websites listed below before they begin their task, and preferably obtain professional advice - librarians are often able to provide guidance. Hunnisett offers detailed advice.

A wide range of indexes are available. Published indexes are listed in the relevant volumes of Raymond's *British*

Indexes (*continued*)

genealogical library guides. An increasing number of indexes to birth, marriages and deaths, the census, monumental inscriptions *etc.* are available on the Family History Online site, and on various other internet sites. Many unpublished indexes are listed in the volumes cited below. See also **Texts and calendars* for indexes published by record societies.

Web Pages:

- Family History Online
  www.familyhistoryonline.net

- **Society of Indexers**
  www.socind.demon.co.uk

- Society of Indexers Genealogical Group
  www.sigg.org.uk

Further Reading:

- GIBSON, JEREMY. & HAMPSON, ELIZABETH. *Specialist indexes for family historians.* 2nd ed. F.F.H.S., 2000.
- JONES, BRIAN. *Index of indexers: a directory showing the location of indexes for the family historian.* 6 pts. Bradford: Brian Jones, 1994-2001.
- HUNNISETT, R. I. *Indexing for editors.* Archives and the user **2.** British Records Association, 1972.

Index Library

The Index Library, published by the British Record Society, includes indexes to a variety of documents, including **Court of Chancery proceedings and **Inquisitions post mortem,* but primarily to the **probate records of numerous ecclesiastical courts. Recently, **hearth tax returns have been added to the series. Full details of these publications are given in **Texts and calendars.*

Web Page:

- The British Record Society 1889-1999
  members.lycos.co.uk/carolyn_busfield/brshist.html

India

The administration of the Raj provided careers for many
Englishmen between the founding of the East India Company
in 1599 and the end of British rule in 1947; for some, it led to
fortunes. Prior to the nineteenth-century, however, few
Englishwomen went there. Some Englishmen married local
girls; most, however returned to England at the end of their
service. Many middle-class families had connections with
India, and it is worth keeping in mind that missing ancestors
may have gone there. The records are in the British
Library's *Oriental and India Office Collections.

India Office Library

See Oriental and India Office Collections

Inheritance

The inheritance customs of England have varied widely over
time and between regions. Primogeniture has been
dominant, but various systems of partible inheritance, e.g.
*gavelkind and *borough english, have also existed. In
practice, however, most parents have always sought to
provide for all their children, and historians now appreciate
that inheritance was a process and not just a single event.
*Wills represented a stage in that process, which commenced
with the first marriage of a child, and only ended with the
death of a widow. A child who was left a token sum of 6d or
so in a will had probably already been established on a farm
or in a trade by his father, who still had to do the same for
other children when he made his will; a testator of yeoman
or higher status who left very little may have retired and
already passed on his property to his children.

Inland Revenue

See Death Duty Registers, and Income Tax

Inns of Court

The Inns of Court provide training for barristers, but were
attended for a time by many gentry who had no intention of

Inns of Court (*continued*)

practising as lawyers. Registers of admissions have been printed and are available in many libraries, for details, see under 'lawyers' in Raymond's *Occupational Sources for genealogists*. 2nd ed., F.F.H.S., 1996.

Inquisitions Post Mortem

In feudal theory, all land was held of the crown. When a tenant in chief (who held directly of the crown) died, his land escheated to the crown.

If there was an heir, he paid a relief to the crown on taking possession; if he was under age, the crown had the right of wardship and marriage, i.e. it was entitled to the revenue of the estate, and to select the heir's bride. These rights could be sold to the highest bidder. The extent of the crown's rights were determined by the holding of an *inquisition post mortem* before a local jury. The resultant *inquisition* give details of lands held, date of death, and the name and age of the heir.

Inquisitions post mortem are now held by the *Public Record Office, amongst the records of the *Court of Chancery (C132), the *Court of Exchequer (E149) and the *Court of Wards and Liveries (WARD 7). They are in Latin. Many have been published, as have various indexes to them. Reference should be made to *Texts and calendars* for *record society publications.

Web Page:

• *Inquisitions post mortem*, Henry III - Charles I: landholders and their heirs
  catalogue.pro.gov.uk/Leaflets/ri2228.htm

Further Reading:

• *Calendar of inquisitions post mortem and other analogous documents preserved in the Public Record Office*. H.M.S.O., 1904-. To be continued. lst series (16 vols.) covers 1235-1392; 2nd series (3 vols.) covers 1485-1509.

- *Index of inquisitions preserved in the Public Record Office.* Lists & indexes **23, 26, 31,** & **33.** Amended ed. New York: Kraus Reprint, 1963. Contents: v.1. Henry VIII to Philip & Mary. v.2. Elizabeth. v.3. James I. v.4. Charles I and later.
- McGUINNESS, MARY. 'Inquisitions post mortem', in STEEL, D. J. *Sources of births, marriages and deaths before 1837 (I).* National index of parish registers 1, Society of Genealogists, 1968, pp.367-71.

Institute of Heraldic & Genealogical Studies

The Institute, located at 79-82, Northgate, Canterbury, Kent CTT 1BA was founded in 1961 as a centre for study and research in family history. It provides training courses and qualifications for professional genealogists, and also runs many other courses. It has an extensive library and publishes a journal, *Family history.* Various other publications are also available.

Web site:
- Institute of Heraldic & Genealogical Studies **www.ihgs.ac.uk**

Insurance Records
See Fire Insurance Records

Interests Lists

Most family history societies publish lists of their members research interests in their journals; these are often updated and published separately. The Federation of Family Histories produces a similar, but much more extensive work, the *Big R.* The *Genealogical research directory,* a commercial publication, provides a similar service. Many interests lists are also available on the internet. All of these lists should be examined by the active researcher; they enable you to make contact with anyone researching the same surnames as yourself, and may lead to extensive information. See also *Guild of One-Name Studies.

Interests Lists (*continued*)
  Web Page:
  • Finding Surname Interests
    www.hawgood.co.uk/finding.htm

International Genealogical Index
The *I.G.I.*, as it is known, is an index to the collection of transcripts and copies of birth / baptism and marriage records held by the Family History Library of the *Church of Jesus Christ of Latter Day Saints. The index covers the entire world, but the U.K. section alone is extensive. It must be remembered that it is only an index; it is always advisable to check the original source, which may reveal additional (or different!) information. Fiche copies of the index are available in many libraries world-wide; it is also available on the web at **www.familysearch.org**

  Other Web Pages:
  • How to use the International Genealogical Index
    www.pro.gov.uk/research/leaflets/igindex.htm
  • Finding LDS Batch Numbers
    www.genuki.org.uk/big/FindingBatchNos.html
  • IGI Batch Numbers
    freepages.genealogy.rootsweb.com/~tyeroots/index4.html

Internet
A vast amount of information for genealogists is now available on the internet. Until recently, this mainly consisted of general advice plus many pages solely devoted to particular families. Now, an increasing number of major databases and indexes are becoming available, as are transcripts of many records - athough the latter tend to be fairly short. It remains the case, however, that very few records have been scanned in direct from the original; consequently, whatever evidence you find on the web should be checked against the original sources if at all possible.

Bear in mind, too, that *books are still far more important in genealogical research than the internet.

Finding information on the internet is not always easy. The use of search engines such as **www.google.com** is liable to produce thousands of irrelevant sites, and it is often better to start with dedicated gateways and portals such as **www.genuki.org.uk** and **www.CyndisList.com**. Raymond's *F.F.H.S. Web directories* series offers printed alternatives to web gateways, which some users will find more convenient.

Genealogical web sites can be categorised into gateways, search engine *etc.,* general introductions, libraries and record offices, family history societies, discussion groups (mailing lists and newsgroups), message / query boards, county pages, surnames, sources, occupational information, professional services (including booksellers), and miscellaneous sites. Some of them are inter-active in character (see *e-mail); most are constantly in a state of flux, continually being up-dated. It is often worth returning to web-sites you have found useful in order to check whether further information has been added.

A major problem in using the internet is that web-site addresses (URL's) frequently change - especially those mounted by individuals. If you cannot find a particular site, it is worth entering distinctive parts of the URL, or words from the title, into a search engine. It may be useful to use the 'advanced search' capabilities of search engines. You may well find that the site sought has moved to a different host, or been given a different URL. Webmasters sometimes preserve the end of a URL when moving a site to a different host.

Further Reading:

- CHRISTIAN, PETER. *The genealogists internet.* Public Record Office, 2001. General introduction.
- RAYMOND, STUART A. *Family history on the web: an internet directory for England and Wales.* 2nd ed., F.F.H.S., 2002. Lists 1,000+ genealogical web-pages.

Interregnum

The period between 1649 and 1660, when there was no king. For part of this period, 1653-58, England was a Protectorate under the rule of Oliver Cromwell and, for 1658-60, his son Richard.

Inventories

See Probate Inventories

Ireland

There has been a great deal of movement between England and Ireland in the last millenium. The 12th century conquest of Ireland led to the settlement of many Anglo-Norman barons and their followers (subsequently known as the 'old English'); the 'plantation' of Ulster under the Tudor and Stuarts led to the migration of many English and Scottish colonists. Many Irish protestants sought refuge in England during the Civil War; even before the Great Famine of the late 1840's, many Irish travelled to England for seasonal work, some of whom suffered transportation to Australia. The famine years saw massive emigration, not just to England but also to North America and elsewhere. Irish migration to England continued into the 20th century; most migrants were labourers, and English records frequently mention them.

General registration of births, marriages and deaths, began in Ireland in 1864, although non-Catholic registration began earlier in 1845. Nineteenth-century census returns have mostly been destroyed; however, returns for the censuses of 1901 and 1911 are available. Griffith's valuation c.1846-65 provide a useful alternative to the census, listing all landowners. The tithe applotment surveys of c.1828-37 are also a useful alternative, listing occupiers of agricultural land. The *Return of owners of land 1873* lists everyone who owned an acre or more of land. Ecclesiastical registers of births, marriages, and deaths, survive from the eighteenth-century, although many Church of Ireland (i.e. Anglican) registers were lost - as were many other records - when the Irish Public Record Office was blown up in 1922. It must be remembered that most of the Irish were Roman Catholic, except in Ulster where many were Presbyterian. Amongst the other records lost in 1922, were wills proved in ecclesiastical courts prior to 1858. District probate registries hold wills proved since that date.

*Passenger lists record the names of many Irish migrants, who can also be traced in the records of the countries to which they migrated. Despite the loss of many records in 1922, it is still possible to trace Irish family history.

Web Pages:
- Genuki Ireland
  www.genuki.org.uk/big.irl

- Ireland Gen Web
  www.irelandgenweb.com/

- Fianna Guide to Irish Genealogy
  www.rootsweb.com/~fianna

Further Reading:
- DAVIS, BILL. *Irish ancestry: a beginners guide.* 3rd ed. F.F.H.S., 2001.
- GRENHAM, JOHN. *Tracing your Irish ancestors.* 2nd ed. Dublin: Gill & Macmillan, 1999.
- RAYMOND, STUART A. *Irish family history on the Web.* F.F.H.S., 2001.

Irregular Marriages
Until Hardwicke's *Marriage Act, 1753, clergy were only permitted to marry those whose banns had been called, or who had a marriage licence. However, failure to comply with these requirements did not invalidate a marriage, and penalties for non-compliance were light. This laxity led to increasing numbers of irregular marriages, and certain churches and other establishments became known for them. Most notorious of all was probably the Fleet Prison in

Irregular Marriages (*continued*)

London, whose chaplains claimed to be outside of the jurisdiction of any bishop: in the 1740's over half of all London weddings took place there. Benton lists surviving registers of the major London marriage centres.

Further Reading:

- BENTON, T. *Irregular marriage in London before 1754.* Society of Genealogists, 1994.

Isle of Man

The Isle of Man is a crown dependency, not part of the United Kingdom; it has its own government, laws and records. Civil registration of marriages commenced in 1849, of births and deaths in 1878. The I.G.I. is virtually complete for Manx registers. The U.K. census includes the island.

Web Pages:

- Isle of Man
  www.isle-of-man.com/interests/genealogy/index.shtml

- A Manx Note Book
  www.ee.surrey.ac.uk/Contrib/manx/

Further Reading:

- NARASIMHAM, JANET. *The Manx family tree: a guide to records in the Isle of Man.* 3rd ed. Isle of Man Family History Society, 2000.

J

Jews

The medieval Jewish community in England was expelled in
1290, and their descendants have not been traced. Most
present-day English Jews are descended from refugees from
Russia, who arrived c. 1880-1914, and from Nazi Germany.
Earlier settlers came from the Iberian peninsula; a variety of
other countries have also contributed to Jewish settlement in
England. Many can be traced in records of *denization and
*naturalization.

Jews may be traced in the usual genealogical sources, and
also in synogogue records, which are often in Hebrew.
Synagogues kept records of Jewish marriage contracts
(Kethubot); there may also be cirumcision registers (kept by
the circumcisor) as well as a variety of other records. These
records will normally still be held by the synagogue.

Web Pages:
- Jewish Genealogical Society of Great Britain
  www.jgsgb.org.uk

- Anglo-Jewish History: Sources in the P.R.O., 18th-20th
  centuries
  catalogue.pro.gov.uk/Leaflets/ri2183.htm

Further Reading:
- MORDY, I. *My ancestors were Jewish: how can I find out
  more about them?* 2nd ed. Society of Genealogists, 1995.
- STEEL, D.J., & SAMUEL, E.R. *Sources for Roman Catholic &
  Jewish genealogy and family history.* National index of
  parish registers 3. Phillimore for the Society of
  Genealogists, 1974.

Journals
See Periodicals

Judicature, Supreme Court of
See Supreme Court of Judicature

Julian Calendar
See Dates

Jurors
The juror is a man sworn, with his fellows, to give a verdict. He may serve at quarter sessions, in a manorial or coroner's court, at an *inquisition post mortem,* and in various other courts; he is likely to be named in the resultant documentation. Liability for jury service at *Quarter sessions and *assizes depended upon a property qualification. Lists of freeholders liable are frequently found with the records of Quarter sessions.

Justices of the Peace
Justices of the Peace (J.Ps.) were first given power to try minor offences in 1361; their powers at *Quarter Sessions were greatly extended under the Tudors. Their names can be found in *Quarter sessions records, in the *liber pacis,* i.e.records of appointment, held by the *Public Record Office for 1571-1921 (class C202), and in the *London gazette,* 1665-1986. Justices occasionally kept their own records of their activities in addition to the official records; some of these have been published.

Further Reading:
- GLEASON, JOHN HOWES. *The Justice of the Peace in England, 1558 to 1640: a later Eirenarcha.* Oxford: Clarendon Press, 1969.
- MOIR, ESTHER. *The Justice of the Peace.* Penguin, 1969.
- MORGAN, GWENDA, & RUSHTON, PETER, eds. *The justicing notebook (1750-64) of Edmund Tew, rector of Boldon.* Surtees Society **205**. 2000.

- QUINTRELL, B. W. ed. *Proceedings of the Lancashire justices of the peace at the sheriffs table during Assizes week, 1578-1694.* Record Society of Lancashire and Cheshire, **121**. 1981.
- PALEY, RUTH, ed. *Justice in eighteenth century Hackney: the justicing notebook of Henry Norris and the Hackney Petty Sessions Book.* London Record Society, **28**. 1991.

K

Kellys Directories
See Trade Directories

Kings Bench
See Court of Kings Bench

Knights
Knights were originally the soldiers who followed William the Conqueror at Hastings, and who were rewarded by grants of land which they held by *knight service. Gradually, the term became honorific and ceased to depend on actual military service; by the seventeenth century, Charles I was able to use the institution of knighthood to fine those who failed to take it up (see *Distraint of Knighthood). Knights frequently headed the leading county families. Knights from 1257 to 1904 are listed in:
- SHAW, W.A. *The Knights of England.* 2 vols. Sherratt & Hughes, 1906.

Knight Service
Knight service was a military tenure by which men held land in return for their service in war. Such land was known as a knight's fee. By the end of the medieval period, knight service had been commuted to a money payment; the tenure was abolished in 1662.

Knighthood, Distraint of
See Distraint of Knighthood

Knight's Fee
Land which would support a knight, held by knight service.

L

Lambeth Palace Library

Lambeth Palace Library, Lambeth Palace, London, SE1 7JU holds many of the archives of the Archbishop of Canterbury. Records of interest to genealogists include a few *bishops' transcripts of the London area, a few original registers and bishops transcripts from overseas churches, records of *marriage licences issued by the *Vicar General and the *Faculty Office, *probate records of some Archbishops' *peculiars, *etc.*, many sources for clergy biography, *estate records, and a wide variety of other sources. Its webpage provides detailed guides to its holdings.

Web Page:
- Lambeth Palace Library
  www.lambethpalacelibrary.org

Land Registry

The Land Registry's register now lists the names of the owners of most property in England and Wales; unfortunately it is not able to provide historical information.

Land Tax

The land tax was introduced in 1692, and only abolished in 1963. It lists, year by year, the names of land-owners and occupiers in each parish. Returns survive in considerable quantity between 1780 and 1832; otherwise, survival is patchy. They are mostly held in county record offices with Quarter sessions records. However, returns for 1798, covering almost all of England and Wales, are in the Public Record Office, class IR23. A full listing of returns is given by Gibson & Medlycott. Surprisingly, few have been published.

Web Page:
- Land Tax Assessments
  www.devon.gov.uk/dra/lta02.html

- Land Tax Assessments for the City of London at Guildhall
  Library
  ihr.sas.ac.uk/gh/landtax.htm

Further Reading:

- GIBSON, J.S.W., MEDLYCOTT, M., & MILLS, D. *Land and window tax assessments.* F.F.H.S., 1993.
- HUNT, H. G. 'Land tax assessments', in MUNBY, L.M. *Short guides to records. First series, 1-24.* [Rev.ed.] Historical Association. 1994, 85-8.
- UNWIN, R.W. *Search guide to the English land tax.* West Yorkshire County Record Office, 1982.
- DAVEY, ROGER, ed. *East Sussex land tax, 1785.* Sussex Record Society **77.** 1991.

Landownership

Land registration has not been popular in England; nor have there been many surveys of land ownership. Consequently, there is no single source which can be consulted to identify landowners, and reliance must be placed on the multifarious records generated by the processes of estate administration (see *estate records) and *taxation. There have been just three general surveys - the eleventh-century *Domesday book, the *return of owners of land of 1873, and Lloyd George's *Valuation Office survey of 1911. *Enclosure awards and *tithe apportionments, both giving names of landowners and tenants, are available for many parishes. Major changes in landownership, however, have taken place - the expropriation of Anglo-Saxon lords by the Normans in 1086 being the most significant, followed in importance by the dissolution of the monasteries and the subsequent sale of their lands by the crown in the sixteenth and early seventeenth centuries. From the late seventeenth until the nineteenth century the trend in landownership was in favour of the big estate; the 1873 survey showed that only 7000 people owned four-fifths of all the land in the United Kingdom. Since then, however, the trend has been towards much wider participation in property ownership - greatly increased under the Thatcher government.

Lathe

The lathe is an administrative unit consisting of a number of hundreds, found in Kent.

Latin

Latin was the language of the law until 1733. It was often also used in *parish registers, *probate records, *etc.,* and is often written in a heavily abbreviated manner. Many of the words used between the eleventh and eighteenth centuries were not known to classical Latin.

Since genealogical research only involves a few Latin records, the vocabulary needed is relatively small, and in some instances identical phraseology will be used repeatedly. Some acquaintance with medieval hand-writing is essential in reading original sources in Latin.

Further Reading:

- STUART, DENIS. *Latin for local and family historians: a beginners guide.* Phillimore, 1995.
- GOODER, EILEEN. *Latin for local history.* 2nd ed. Longman, 1978.
- MARTIN, CHARLES TRICE. *The record interpreter: a collection of abbreviations, Latin words and names used in English historical manuscripts and records.* 2nd ed. Steven & Sons, 1910. Reprinted in facsimile, Phillimore, 1982.
- PARKER, JOHN. *Reading Latin epitaphs: a handbook for beginners.* Penzance: Cressor Publications, 1999.

Latter Day Saints

See Church of Jesus Christ of Latter Day Saints

Lay Subsidy

The lay subsidy was a tax on the moveable personal wealth of individuals, rather than on their land. Returns listing taxpayers survive from c.1290-1332, and from c.1522 to the mid-seventeenth century. This was the major Parliamentary tax of the period; returns survive in the *Public Record Office, class E179. Returns after the mid-sixteenth century list increasingly fewer names. Many lay subsidies have been published; these are listed in the county volumes of Raymond's *British genealogical library guides,* and in *Texts and calendars.*

Web Page:

- Taxation Records before 1660
  catalogue.pro.gov.uk/Leaflets/ri2117.htm

Further Reading:

- HOYLE, R.W. *Tudor taxation records: a guide for users.* P.R.O. users guide, **5.,** 1994.
- *Exchequer K. R. lay subsidy rolls (E179).* List and Index Society, **44, 54, 63, 75 & 87.** 1969-73.
- LANG, R.G., ed. *Two Tudor subsidy assessment rolls for the City of London, 1541 and 1582.* London Record Society **29.** 1992.
- HOYLE, R.W., ed. *Early Tudor Craven subsidies and assessments 1510-1547.* Yorkshire Archaeological Society record series **145.** 1987.

Lease and Release

The lease and release was a method of conveyancing intended to avoid *livery of seizin or enrolment on a *court roll. The purchaser first took a one-year lease of the property; the vendor, on the following day, granted the reversion of the lease to the purchaser.

Leasehold

Land held by lease was held for a specified period. The three-life or 99 year lease was common c.1550-1750; shorter leases became usual in the late eighteenth century. The 'perpetual' lease, granted for a very long period, e.g. 1,000 years, was virtually a sale of the property. Building leases, generally for 99 years, required the tenant to build a house.

The three-life lease is of particular value to genealogists, since it is likely to name several family members, i.e. the tenant himself, and those most likely to live for a long time. It usually required payment of an *entry fine, as well as rent, and the tenant could assign it to another tenant, or sub-let the property. Endorsements on leases may enable successive tenants of the property to be identified.

Letters Close
See Close Rolls

Letters of Administration
See Administration Bonds

Letters Patent
See Patent Rolls

Liberty
A manor or other area exempt from a sheriff's jurisdiction.

Libraries
Libraries are vital sources of information for genealogists. They are warehouses of *books, *periodicals and *microfiche; they also sometimes hold *manuscript materials.

Most genealogists will be familiar with public libraries before they start their research, although they may not have ventured into the *local studies library. There are a variety of other libraries also likely to be of value. University libraries often have extensive runs of English *record society publications and county historical journals. *Family history societies usually have libraries, which increasingly are housed in their own premises rather than in members' homes. *The Society of Genealogist has the major library solely devoted to family history in England. The *British

Libraries (*continued*)

Library has one of the most extensive genealogical collections in the country; national libraries in other countries, e.g. the *Library of Congress and the Australian National Library, also have extensive British genealogical collections. Many county historical and archaeological societies have runs of county historical journals exchanged with other county societies; some, e.g. the Yorkshire Archaeological Society, have extensive genealogical collections. The *Family History Centers of the *Church of Jesus Christ of Latter Day Saints provide access to the resources of the church's Family History Library in Utah. Each library has its own particular strengths, and it is worth finding out what these are. Any reference librarian should be able to advise you in the use of their own library, and identify other libraries likely to hold other useful material. Do not be hesitant about asking librarians for advice: it is their job to give it!

Most libraries now have web-sites, which should be checked for details of their holdings and opening hours (the latter change surprisingly frequently). Many have web-based catalogues. Unless you intend to rely on serendipity (fun, but very wasteful of time, and often ineffective), you will need to consult library catalogues. But, first, it is necessary to identify the particular books you need. Many are mentioned in this volume, but you really need to consult detailed *bibliographies in order to appreciate the extent of the resources available to you, and to identify the particular books it would be useful to consult. Once you have done this, you can go to library catalogues to locate them. Even if the book you require is not available in a local library, you may be able to borrow it via inter-library loan.

Web Pages:

- Familia: the U.K. and Ireland's Guide to Genealogical Sources in Public Libraries
  www.familia.org.uk

- OBI-OPACS in Britain and Ireland
  www.niss.ac.uk/lis/obi/obi.htm
  Directory of library catalogues and services

Further Reading:
- RAYMOND, STUART A. *Using libraries: workshops for family historians.* F.F.H.S., 2001.

Library of Congress

The Library of Congress is the largest library in the world, and holds an extensive collection of British genealogical materials. It should not be ignored by American researchers.

Web Site:
- Library of Congress Local History & Genealogy Reading Room
  www.loc.gov/rr/genealogy/

Licences

Licences have been required by the subjects of the crown for a whole host of reasons. Schoolmasters, midwives, physicians and surgeons needed licences from their bishop to practise; records of these are preserved with diocesan records. Victuallers had to be licensed by *Quarter sessions, as did badgers, drovers, and other itinerant tradesmen. Non-conformist meeting houses required licences in the seventeenth and eighteenth centuries. *Passports originated as 'licences to pass beyond the seas'. In the twentieth century, everyone became familiar with motor vehicle licences (See *Vehicle registration).

The evidence provided by official records of these licences, can be very helpful to the family historian. They enable us to locate ancestors in time and place, and tell us something of their activities.

List and Index Society

The List and Index Society publishes lists and indexes of documents in the *Public Record Office such as state papers,

List and Index Society (*continued*)

tax lists, court records, accounts, *etc., etc.* Its publications are available in most major reference libraries. The society continues the work of the *List & index* series, formerly published by the *Public Record Office, runs of which are also widely available.

Livery Companies

The livery companies are the guilds of the City of London, many of which have been in continuous existence since medieval times. Originally they regulated trade and traders in their particular 'mysteries', and were closely linked with city government. By the eighteenth-century, they were becoming major charitable institutions whose members did not necessarily have any links to the particular trade of their company.

Company records contain much of interest to genealogists, - especially records of *apprentices and admission to the freedom of the company, but also their *estate records, minutes of proceedings, *etc.*

Further Reading:

• GUILDHALL LIBRARY. *City Livery companies and related organisations: a guide to their archives in Guildhall Library.* 3rd ed. Guildhall Library. 1989.

Many relevant books and journal articles are listed in:
• RAYMOND, STUART A. *Londoner's occupations: a genealogical guide.* 2nd ed., F.F.H.S., 2001.

Livery of Seizin

The ritual by which land was conveyed in medieval times, involving the handing over of a symbol of the property - a clod of earth, or a key - in the presence of witnesses.

Local History

Local history and *family history are closely related. The family historian needs to be able to set his ancestors in the context of the society in which he lived - generally a local context - and thus depends on the work of the local historian. The two disciplines rely on many of the same sources, but apply different methods to them. Family historians need an understanding of the ways in which local historians use *wills, *parish registers, the records of *taxation, *etc.,* to build up pictures of local society. They need to read local histories of the communities in which their ancestors lived. They need to use unusual local sources which local historians may have identified. Their interest in ensuring that sources are easily available is identical.

Conversely, local historians need the work genealogists do in transcribing sources such as *parish registers and *monumental inscriptions. They need their support in lobbying for improved access to libraries and archives. The writing of family history easily merges into the writing of local history.

Web Pages:
- Sources for Local History
  www.hmc.gov.uk/focus/text/localsourcestxt.htm

- Local History at the Public Record Office
  www.pro.gov.uk/pathways/localhistory/intro.htm

Further Reading:
- HOSKINS, W. G. *Local history in England.* 3rd. ed. Longman, 1984.
- RIDEN, PHILIP. *Record sources for local history.* B.T. Batsford, 1987.
- HEY, DAVID, ed. *The Oxford companion to local and family history.* Oxford University Pres,, 1996.
- RICHARDSON, JOHN. *The local historians encyclopaedia.* 2nd ed. Historical Publications, 1989.
- FRIAR, STEPHEN. *The local history companion.* Rev. ed. Stroud: Sutton, 2001.
- TILLER, KATE. *English local history: an introduction.* Rev. ed. Stroud. Sutton, 2002.

Local Studies Libraries

Virtually all public library authorities in the U.K. accept their responsibility for assembling a comprehensive collection of publications relating to their own area. Normally, the collection will include local books, the journals and transactions of county, local and *family history societies, the publications of local *record societies, back runs of local *newspapers, any microfiche/film published by local family history societies, local *trade directories and gazetteers, printed maps, local acts of Parliament, and various other ephemera. There may also be some manuscript material, e.g. many family history societies deposit transcripts of *monumental inscriptions in local studies libraries. *Archives, however, will normally be in the county record office - unless libraries and archives have been combined in one institution, as at the Surrey History Centre. See also *libraries.

Further Reading:

• WINTERBOTHAM, DIANA. & CROSBY, ALAN. *The local studies library: a handbook for local historians.* British Association for Local History, 1998.

London gazette

This is the official publication of the Crown, first issued in 1665/6, and issued regularly ever since. It publishes official notices on a wide variety of topics, including many likely to be of interest to genealogists. For example, senior appointments in the civil service, the armed forces, and the church appear regularly. Bankrupts and insolvent debtors are listed, as are naturalized aliens and persons who change their name.

The *London gazette* is available in major reference libraries; full runs are held at the British Library and Guildhall Library. The web page includes full text from 1900, and is fully indexed.

Web Page:
- Gazette Online
  www.gazettes-online.co.uk

Lord Hardwicke's Marriage Act
See Marriage Act 1753

Lord Lieutenants
The office of Lord Lieutenant was created in the mid-sixteenth century to take command of the militia in each county. Most surviving records of their activities date from the late eighteenth and early nineteenth centuries, and include some nominal lists of militiamen. These may be found in county record offices, see *Militia Records.

Further Reading:
- DUNN, RICHARD MINTA, ed. *Norfolk Lieutenancy journal, 1660-1676.* Norfolk Record Society **45**. 1977.
- GORING, JEREMY, & WAKE, JOAN, eds. *Northamptonshire lieutenancy papers and other documents 1580-1614.* Northamptonshire Record Society **1975. 27.** 1975.

M

Mailing Lists
> *See* E-mail

Manors
> The manor was the prime unit in estate administration, and also played an important role in local government until the end of the medieval period. Manorial records may survive from the twelfth century until as late as 1925 (when copyhold tenure was abolished), although complete runs of *court rolls for the whole period are rare (the rolls of the manor of Wakefield are a notable exception to this rule).
>
> The manorial court, presided over by the lord or his steward, governed manorial administration. It met at regular intervals, depending on local custom; the matters it dealt with were both judicial and administrative. The *court baron regulated the manor's agriculture, the respective rights and duties of lord and tenants, tenurial changes, and disputes between tenants; the *court leet and view of frankpledge dealt with the election of officers, e.g. the reeve, the constable, (etc.) and police matters such as breaches of the peace and other felonies.
>
> The proceedings of the court were recorded on *court rolls, which contain a great deal of information of value to the genealogist. In particular, it is possible to trace the descent of properties from father to son, and consequently the court rolls can be used as a substitute for *parish registers where the latter are not available - especially in the medieval period.
>
> Other manorial records include *rentals, *accounts, *surveys, custumals (recording customary rights and duties), *maps, *etc.* Most are in *Latin until the mid-eighteenth

century, although much phraseology is used repeatedly, and is easy to learn. These records are to be found in a variety of repositories; they are likely to be in the local *county record office or the *Public Record Office; in case of doubt, the Historical Manuscripts Commission's Manorial Documents Register should be consulted. Bear in mind that many manorial records have perished.

Web Pages:
- Manor and other local court rolls, 13th century - 1922
  catalogue.pro.gov.uk/Leaflets/ri2227.htm

- Manorial Records in the Public Record Office
  catalogue.pro.gov.uk/Leaflets/ri2219.htm

- Manorial Documents Register
  www.hmc.gov.uk/mdr/mdr.htm

Further Reading:
- ELLIS, MARY. *Using manorial records.* 2nd ed. Readers guide **6**. Public Record Office, 1997.
- HARVEY, P.D.A. *Manorial Records.* Archives and the user **5**. British Records Association, 1984.
- STUART, D. *Manorial records: an introduction to their transcription and translation.* Phillimore, 1992.

Manuscripts
Documents which have not been published, usually hand-written. *Archives are usually manuscripts, but the term also embraces unpublished transcripts of e.g. monumental inscriptions and parish registers, the original manuscripts from which books were type-set, *etc.* Care should be taken in handling manuscripts, since they are generally unique documents (although some may exist in several copies), and consequently irreplaceable.

Maps
Maps have a variety of uses for family historians. Firstly, some knowledge of English topography, and the ability to

Maps (*continued*)

locate particular places - especially parishes - is essential for identifying parish registers and other sources that may be worth searching. *Phillimore's atlas and index* provides invaluable maps of parish boundaries, juxtaposed with nineteenth century topographical maps, which will help you to locate your ancestors' homes, and identify adjacent parishes. Individual county maps of parish boundaries are available from the *Institute of Heraldic and Genealogical Studies. Early large scale Ordnance Survey maps provide very detailed information on parochial topography as our ancestors would have known it. You may need modern large scale Ordnance Survey maps if you want to visit particular houses and farms. Gazetteers will help you locate places which may occur in original sources.

*Tithe maps, *enclosure award maps, and maps associated with the *national farm survey of 1941-3, and the *Valuation Office survey of 1909 provide more direct information. The lists of owners and occupiers that are usually found with such maps may provide useful information on your ancestors, locating them in time and place, and providing detailed descriptions of the property they owned or occupied. Estate maps may also give names of tenants, *etc.*

Further Reading:

- HUMPHERY-SMITH, C.R. *The Phillimore atlas and index of parish registers.* 2nd ed. Phillimore, 1995.
- HARLEY, J.B. & PHILLIPS, C.W. *The historians guide to Ordnance Survey maps.* National Council of Social Service for the Standing Conference for Local History, 1964.
- HINDLE, PAUL. *Maps for local history.* B.T. Batsford, 1988.
- OLIVER, RICHARD. *Ordnance Survey maps: a concise guide for historians.* The Charles Close Society, 1993.
- OLIVER, RICHARD. 'Ordnance Survey maps', in THOMPSON, K.M., ed. *Short guides to records. Second series guides, 25-48.* Historical Association, 1997, 83-6.

Marriage

Marriage in England was originally based on the common law requirement that there be mutual consent and agreement to a lifelong union. Witnesses, ceremonies, clergy, *etc.*, were not legally required. By the seventeenth-century, however, most marriages took place in church - although it was not until Lord Hardwick's *Marriage Act of 1753 that common law marriage ceased to be recognised. Until then, many marriages were valid at common law despite the fact that they had been contracted in a manner contrary to canon law.

Weddings in churches were recorded in *parish registers from their commencement in 1538. There was a brief hiatus between 1653 and 1660, when marriages were conducted by justices of the peace.

After the Restoration, the number of irregular marriages gradually increased. Hardwick's Act ended this practise, and considerably tightened up the conditions under which marriage was considered legally valid. It also improved the information provided in parish registers.

It was not until 1837 that civil marriage again became legal; the Civil Registration Act of 1836 provided that registrars could issue licences for marriage in either registrar's offices, or in nonconformist chapels.

Further Reading:

- CHAPMAN, COLIN R. *Marriage laws, rites, records and customs.* Dursley: Lochin Publishing, 1996.
- GILLIS, JOHN R. *For better, for worse: British marriages 1600 to the present.* Oxford University Press, 1985.

Marriage Act, 1753

Popularly known as Lord Hardwicke's Act, this ended the practise of common law marriage before two witnesses. Marriage could henceforth only take place after the publication of *banns (which had to be entered in a separate register) or on the production of a valid *marriage licence. It had to be performed by an Anglican clergyman in the parish

Marriage Act, 1753 (*continued*)

church of one of the spouses. The only exemptions from this requirement were for Jews and Quakers; other nonconformist marriages only became legal again in 1837, when *civil registration was introduced. Minors had to have the consent of their parents or guardians. The act also required more detailed marriage entries in parish registers.

Hardwicke's act was intended to end the scandal of irregular marriages. Henceforth, couples who wanted to elope sought a border marriage.

Marriage Certificate

See Civil Registration

Marriage Duty Act 1695

This act imposed a duty on births, marriages and burials, and on bachelors and childless widowers. Assessments were partly based on *parish registers, and probably caused a reduction in the number of events they recorded. Assessment required a complete enumeration of the population. Unfortunately, few assessments and enumerations survive. The act was abolished in 1706.

Further Reading:

- GLASS, D.V., ed. *London inhabitants within the walls, 1695.* London Record Society **2**. 1966.
- RALPH, ELIZABETH, & WILLIAMS, MARY E., eds. *The inhabitants of Bristol in 1696.* Bristol Record Society publications **25**. 1968.

Marriage Indexes

Many indexes to marriage entries in *parish registers and *bishops transcripts, and to marriage licences, are now available. The *International genealogical index is the most comprehensive, although it is far from being complete. *Boyds marriage index covers 16 counties throughout England; *Pallots index covers mainly London and Middlesex. Many *family history societies have indexed marriage registers in their own localities, some of which have been published as *books, *microfiche or *CD. Other indexes may be found in *family history society libraries, or in their compiler's possession; sometimes a search fee is payable.

It is usually desirable to note all index entires relating to a particular surname; otherwise, you may need to consult an index again. It should also be remembered that the index is not the original register; the latter should always be consulted, as it may contain additional information, and consultation acts as a check on the accuracy of the index.

Further Reading:
* GIBSON, JEREMY, & HAMPSON, ELIZABETH. *Marriage and census indexes for family historians.* 8th ed. F.F.H.S., 2000.

Marriage Licences
A marriage licence exempted the parties concerned from the requirement to have *banns called, and thus enabled them to marry quickly, or to avoid the indignity of banns. It could be obtained from the chancellor or surrogate of the diocese in which either of the parties lived, or from the officers of the Archbishops of York and Canterbury. Few licences have survived; however, one of the parties, usually the bridegroom, had to make a statement - an allegation - to the effect that there was no impediment to the proposed marriage. This allegation normally included the names, ages, occupations and places of residence of the couple, and whether they were single or widowed; it also noted the place of the proposed marriage. Until 1823, a bond was also required; this also gave the names of the parties. Marriage allegations and bonds are to be found in the relevant diocesan record office; a number of indexes to them have been published, and are listed in the county volumes of Raymond's *British genealogical library guides* series. An index to those issued by the *Vicar-General and *Faculty Office of the Province of Canterbury is available on the internet.

Marriage Licences (*continued*)

A word of warning: just because a licence was issued, it does not necessarily follow that a marriage took place.

Web Page:

• Marriage Licence Allegations Index 1694-1850: Vicar-General and Faculty Office
  www.englishorigins.com/help/mla-details.aspx

Further Reading:

• GIBSON, JEREMY. *Bishops transcripts and marriage licences, bonds and allegations: a guide to their location and indexes.* 5th ed. F.F.H.S., 2001.

• 'Marriage licences', in STEEL, D.J., *et al. Sources of births, marriages and deaths before 1837 (I).* National index of parish registers 1. Society of Genealogists, 1968, 223-44.

• DUNKIN, EDWIN H.W., ed. *Calendar of Sussex Marriage licences recorded in the Consistory Court of the Bishop of Chichester for the Archdeaconry of Lewes, August 1586 to March 1642-3.* Sussex Record Society, 1. 1901.

Marriage Settlement

Marriage settlements conveyed property to the use of the parties, providing for the children of the marriage and for the survivor after the death of one spouse. They identify the original owner of the property conveyed, frequently the parents, and may name other relatives as trustees.

Matrimonial Causes Act

See Divorce

Medals

Medals were first introduced in the nineteenth century, and have been awarded for campaigns or particular battles, for good conduct or long service, and for gallantry. Medal rolls are held in the *Public Record Office, mainly amongst the War Office archives. Gallantry awards are published in the *London gazette.

Web Pages:

- British Armed Services: Campaign Medals and other Service Medals
  catalogue.pro.gov.uk/Leaflets/ri2296.htm

- British Armed Services: Gallantry Medals
  catalogue.pro.gov.uk/Leaflets/ri2297.htm

- Civilian Gallantry Medals
  catalogue.pro.gov.uk/Leaflets/ri2120.htm

Medieval Genealogy

It is not easy to trace ancestors in the period prior to the introduction of parish registers. Most of the records that survive relate to the landowning classes - although a good run of manorial *court rolls may enable villein families to be traced. *Inquisitions post mortem* provide the easiest means to trace tenants in chief; *title deeds enable the genealogists to trace the descent of particular properties, *lay subsidy assessments list tax-payers; *wills may identify relatives. Many sources have been published, and are listed in the county volumes of Raymond's *British Genealogical Library Guides* series. There are few genealogists able to identify an ancestor in *Domesday book, but the possibility is always there!

Web Sites:

- Medieval and Early Modern Sources for Family History
  catalogue.pro.gov.uk/Leaflets/ri2112.htm

- Some Notes on Medieval English genealogy
  www.medievalgenealogy.org.uk

Further Reading:

- FRANKLIN, PETER. *Some medieval records for family historians: an introduction to the purposes, contents and interpretation of pre-1538 records available in print.* F.F.H.S., 1994.

Meeting Houses

Non-conformist chapels are frequently termed meeting houses in early records. From 1689 until the early nineteenth century, they required licences, which provide names of prominent dissenters.

Further Reading:

- CHANDLER, J.H., ed. *Wiltshire dissenters meeting house certificates and registrations, 1689-1852.* Wiltshire Record Society **40**. 1985.

Members Interests

See Interests Lists

Memorial Inscriptions

See Monumental Inscriptions

Methodists

The Methodist denominations followed the teaching of the Wesley brothers, and finally split from the Church of England in 1784. Various splinter groups - the Methodist New Connexion, Wesleyan Methodists, Primitve Methodists, Bible Christians, United Methodists, *etc.* - established their own churches, but most came back together in the early twentieth century.

Methodists accepted Church of England baptism, marriage and burial ceremonies, and do not have many early registers. In 1837 many of those which had been kept were deposited with the Registrar General, and are now in the *Public Record Office, class RG4. Baptismal registers are more frequent than marriage and burial registers; they belonged to circuits rather than particular chapels. Circuits sometimes changed boundaries, and genealogists may need to search the registers of neighbouring circuits. Later registers are in *county record offices, or may still be with ministers. Other circuit records are also frequently deposited in county record offices.

From 1778, the various denominations published journals which included death notices and obituaries. Many of these, together with the minutes of conference (containing ministerial biographies), and much other archival and published materials, are held at the Methodist Archives and Research Centre, John Rylands Library, Deansgate, Manchester M3 3EH.

Web Page:
- Methodist Archives and Research Centre
  rylibweb.man.ac.uk/datal/dg/text/method.html

Further Reading:
- LEARY, W. *My ancestors were Methodist: how can I find out more about them?* ed. M. Gandy. New ed. Society of Genealogists, 1991.
- 'The Methodists', in STEEL, D.J. *Sources for nonconformist genealogy and family history.* National index of parish registers **2.** Society of Genealogists, 1973, 721-40.
- COSTEN, M.D., ed. *Wesleyans and Bible Christians in South Somerset: accounts and minutes 1808-1907.* Somerset Record Society **78.** 1984.

Microfiche
Microfiche offers a cheap means of publishing information which would be too expensive to print. It is used extensively by family history societies to produce indexes and transcripts of *parish registers, *monumental inscriptions, *census returns, *etc.* Many commercial publishers have used it to reprint *trade directories, *record society publications, and similar works. Comprehensive listings of microfiche currently available are provided by:
- PERKINS, JOHN. *Current publications on microfiche by member societies.* 5th ed. F.F.H.S., 2002. Also available on CD.
- RAYMOND, STUART A. *British genealogical microfiche.* F.F.H.S., 1999.

165

Migration

It is now recognised that most of our ancestors lived in various different places at different times in their lives. In rural areas, most teenagers left home early to work as a living-in servant in a household which might be five or ten miles distant from their parents' home; it was quite normal for such servants to move masters every year or two, travelling similar distances to do so. Some would be attracted to big cities like London, which was home to many long-distance migrants. Those most likely to stay in the same parish were the men who had a stake in local society, the yeoman farmers and their eldest sons.

Tracing mobile ancestors is not always easy. But it can be done! Many genealogical sources provide clues: *wills might request burial in a different parish from that in which the testator lived; marriage registers often identify the parishes from which spouses came; settlement certificates provide mini-biographies for the poorer members of society; the *census gives places of birth.

Further Reading:

• CAMP, A.J. *My ancestor moved in England and Wales.* Society of Genealogists, 1994.

Militia Records

The Militia Act of 1757 created militia regiments in every English county, reviving a tradition of universal service which had fallen into desuetude after the seventeenth-century civil war (see *Muster Rolls). Recruitment was by ballot: constables drew up lists of all the able-bodied men aged between 18 and 50 in their parish, and drew lots to decide who should either serve or pay for a replacement. There were certain exemptions, and liability for service for those over 45 was ended in 1762.

The militia ballot lists for 1757-1831 should theoretically be almost full censuses of able-bodied men. In practice, they are not; nevertheless, they are valuable sources for genealogists. Similar documents include the *posse comitatus* lists of 1798, and the *levee en masse* lists of 1803-4.

Muster rolls, listing those actually chosen to serve, are more frequent survivals, and may also be of use to family historians, especially where they identify parishes.

Web Page:
- Militia Records 1757-1914
  www.pro.gov.uk/leaflets/ri2018.htm

Further Reading:
- SPENCER, WILLIAM. *Records of the Militia and Volunteer forces from 1757.* Public Record Office readers guide **3**. 1993
- GIBSON, JEREMY, & MEDLYCOTT, MERVYN. *Militia lists and musters 1757-1876: a directory of holdings in the British Isles.* 4th ed. F.F.H.S., 2000.
- HATLEY, VICTOR A., ed. *Northamptonshire militia lists 1777.* Northamptonshire Record Society, **25**. 1973.

Missing Persons
A number of agencies are dedicated to tracing missing persons. The Salvation Army's Family tracing service seeks to restore family relationships by locating relatives, although it will not act merely to trace genealogies. The Red Cross works world-wide to trace relatives who have lost contact due to war or natural disaster; of particular interest to genealogists are its records of the Second World War. The National Missing Persons Helpline works to provide support both for 'missing persons' and their families, and seeks to re-unite them. Many genealogical inquiries for missing persons are posted at the 'missing you' web-site. There are many commercial tracing services available on the internet.

Web Pages:
- Look 4 Them
  www.look4them.org.uk
  Gateway to web-sites of organizations

- National Missing Persons Helpline
  www.missingpersons.org

- Family Tracing Service
  www.salvationarmy.org.uk/familytracing/

- British Red Cross
  www.redcross.org.uk

- Missing Persons
  www.missing-you/index.htm

- Reunite
  www.reunite.co.uk

Further Reading:
- ROGERS, C.D. *Tracing missing persons: an introduction to agencies, methods and sources in England and Wales.* 2nd ed. Manchester: Manchester University Press, 1985.

Monumental Brasses
See Brasses

Monumental Inscriptions

The practice of erecting monumental (or memorial) inscriptions (M.I's) began in earnest in the sixteenth century. Older memorials - brasses, effigies, *etc.* - are few, and generally commemorate members of the gentry and baronial classes. Inscriptions often give more information than parish register entries; where possible both should be checked and compared.

Most *family history societies have been busy transcribing memorials, frequently depositing copies in *county record offices, *local studies libraries, and/or the *Society of Genealogists, as well as in their own libraries. They have published many transcripts and indexes as *books or *microfiche, as have a number of other publishers. The county volumes of Raymond's *British genealogical library* *guides* should be consulted for published inscriptions. Many inscriptions are also available on the internet, and have been listed in Raymond's directory.

Web Page:
- Monumental Inscriptions for Genealogists
  www.neep.demon.co.uk/mis/
  How to record them

Further Reading:
- RAYMOND, STUART A. *Monumental inscriptions on the web: a directory.* F.F.H.S., 2002.
- COLLINS, L., *et al. Monumental inscriptions in the library of the Society of Genealogists.* 2 vols. Society of Genealogists, 1984-7.
- 'Monumental inscriptions', in STEEL, D.J., *et al. Sources of births, marriages and deaths before 1837 (I).* National index of parish registers 1. Society of Genealogists, 1968, 245-70.
- RAYMENT, JOHN L. *Rayment's notes on recording monumental inscriptions,* rev. Penelope Pattinson. 4th ed. F.F.H.S., 1992.
- PARKER, JOHN. *Reading Latin epitaphs: a handbook for beginners.* Penzance: Cressar Publications, 1999.

Mormons
This is the popular name for members of the Church of Jesus Christ of Latter-Day Saints. The book of Mormon is their sacred book.

Mortuary
A mortuary was a payment made to the incumbent clergyman on the death of a parishioner. It may also refer to any building to which the dead were brought.

Muster Rolls
The militia originated as the Anglo-Saxon fyrd, which demanded military service from every able-bodied man. The requirement for military service remained in place until the

Muster Rolls *(continued)*

twentieth century. Under the Tudors and Stuarts, the militia was mustered frequently and many muster rolls were compiled listing able-bodied men in each parish. Some of these muster rolls have been published; many others remain in manuscript, in the *Public Record Office and elsewhere. See *militia records for eighteenth and nineteenth century records.

Further Reading:
- GIBSON, JEREMY, & DELL, ALAN. *Tudor and Stuart muster rolls: a directory of holdings in the British Isles.* 2nd ed. F.F.H.S., 1989.
- CHIBNALL. A.C., ed. *The certificates of musters for Buckinghamshire in 1522.* Buckinghamshire Record Society, 17. 1973.

N

Name Lists

A wide variety of name lists are available to the genealogist. Those which cover large areas, such as counties, and which identify the parishes in which individuals lived, are particularly useful, since they provide a means of locating the homes of family names. Such lists include *taxation returns, *electoral registers, *poll books, the *protestation returns of 1641/2, *militia records, and the *census. Many transcripts and indexes of these and other lists have been published; such publications can be identified in the county volumes of Raymond's *British genealogical library guides.*

National Archives

See Historical Manuscript Commission, and Public Record Office.

National Army Museum

This Museum is devoted to the history of the British Army from 1485 to the present day. In addition to its exhibits; it also has an extensive library, with many diaries and letters of soldiers and officers, and other manuscript materials. The address is Royal Hospital Road, Chelsea, London SW3 4HT.

Web Page:
- National Army Museum
  www.national-army-museum.ac.uk

National Farm Survey

The urgent need to increase food production at the beginning of World War II meant that the authorities needed information on the resources available to them. A brief survey of agricultural land was conducted in 1940; a more

National Farm Survey (*continued*)

extended survey followed in 1941-3. The records include surveys of every farm and holding of over five acres, giving full details of the conditions of tenure, and length of occupancy, crop acreage, livestock, farm equipment, and farm management, including the name of the farmer.

Each holding is mapped. The records provide an invaluable census of land-ownership in the mid-twentieth century, and may help to fill in your family history if you know where your family had a holding.

Web Page:
- National Farm Surveys of England and Wales 1940-1943
  catalogue.pro.gov.uk/Leaflets/ri2271.htm

Further Reading:
- FOOT, WILLIAM. *Maps for family history: a guide to the records of the tithe, Valuation Office, and national farm surveys of England and Wales 1836-1943.* Public Record Office readers guide **9.** 1994.

National Library of Wales

The National Library of Wales, Aberystwyth, Dyfed SY23 3BU, is entitled to a copy of every book published in the U.K. Its archival collections are extensive, including the records of the *Court of Great Sessions, many Welsh *parish registers, *bishops' transcripts, marriage bonds, other *diocesan records, *estate records, *etc.* Catalogues of both books and archives are available on-line, although the latter is not yet complete.

Web Pages:
- National Library of Wales
  www.llgc.org.uk

Further Reading:
- *A guide to genealogical sources at the National Library of Wales.* Aberystwyth: National Library of Wales, Dept. of Manuscripts and Records, 1986.

National Register of Archives

The Historical Manuscripts Commission's National Register of Archives consists of over 43,000 unpublished lists of archival and manuscript collections, which are indexed on the N.R.A.'s web page. The indexes serve as a location register for collections held in record offices throughout the country. The indexes available are not designed primarily with the genealogist in mind, but may lead to sources likely to contain genealogical information. The 'family and estate' index only lists families whose *estate records are listed. The 'personal' index is an index of prominent individuals whose papers have been listed. The 'organisation index' and the 'business index' can be searched by the names of organizations (such as churches or charities) or businesses, or by place - but the latter search will only lead to those which are based in the place searched. They will not show branches or operations conducted in other places. Searchers should read the web-page descriptions of these indexes before they search.

Web Page:
• National Register of Archives
www.hmc.gov.uk/nra/nra2.htm

Naturalisation

Prior to 1844, aliens could only be naturalized by act of Parliament. The original private bills of naturalization are in the House of Lords Record Office. Most aliens therefore, sought denization rather than naturalization. After 1844, naturalization could be granted by a certificate from the Home Secretary. Copies of certificates are enrolled on the Close rolls for 1844-73; from 1874 to 1969 they are in class HO334 in the Public Record Office. Yearly indexes can be found in the *Parliamentary papers, available in many reference libraries. See also *immigrants and aliens, and *denization.

Naturalization (*continued*)

Web Page:
- Grants of British Nationality
  catalogue.pro.gov.uk/Leaflets/ri2156.htm

New Poor Law
   See Poor Law

Newspapers
   Birth, marriage and death notices in newspapers are
   important sources of information, as are the detailed
   accounts of weddings which frequently occurred in local
   newspapers. *Obituaries are also useful; newspapers also
   have accounts of significant moments in our ancestors lives,
   e.g. robberies, *coroners inquests, advertisements, disasters,
   runaway apprentices, *etc., etc.*

   Few newspapers apart from the *Times* are indexed; those
   indexes which are available are listed by both Chapman and
   Gibson, *et al.* The British Library's Newspaper Library at
   Colindale has extensive runs of local newspapers; many are
   also to be found in local studies libraries. The library is also
   involved with the Newsplan project, which is a co-operative
   programme for microfilming and preserving old newspapers,
   and which has published many union lists, giving locations
   of those which survive.

Web Page:
- The British Library Newspaper Library
  www.bl.uk/collections/newspapers.html

Further Reading:
- CHAPMAN, COLIN R. *Using newspapers and periodicals.* An
  introduction to ... series. F.F.H.S., 1993.
- GIBSON, JEREMY, LANGSTONE, BRETT, & SMITH, BRENDA W.
  *Local newspapers 1750-1920: England and Wales; Channel
  Islands; Isle of Man: a select location list.* 2nd ed. F.F.H.S.,
  2002.

New Zealand

British settlement of New Zealand commenced in 1790. It was originally governed from New South Wales, but became a crown colony in 1840. Civil registration of European births, marriages and deaths, commenced in 1848, becoming compulsory in 1856. A high percentage of the early immigrants are mentioned in land records, since the offer of land was an incentive for them to immigrate. The National Archives and local land registries hold extensive records. Large numbers of passenger lists also survive in the National Archives and elsewhere. Wills, since 1842, are mostly held in the National Archives; census returns have not survivied; the New Zealand Society of Genealogists is publishing transcriptions of monumental inscriptions and some burial records. The originals of the latter are either still with the incumbent, or with the diocesan archives.

Web Pages:

- New Zealand Society of Genealogists
  www.genealogy.org.nz

- Genealogical Sources [at Archives New Zealand]
  **www.archives.govt.nz/holdings/research/
  genealogical/genealogical_sources_frame.html**

Further Reading:

- BROMELL, ANNE. *Tracing family history in New Zealand.* Godwit, 1996.
- KALOPULU, KAREN, & DEANNE, ROSEMARY. *Researching family history in the collections of Auckland City Libraries.* 5th ed. Auckland Public Library, 1997.

Nicknames

Nicknames, diminutives, and pet-names came before *surnames; indeed, many of the latter are derived from the former. The genealogist needs to be on the lookout for their use: Tony for Antony, Bill for William, Marion for Mary, Aggie for Agnes, Jack for John, *etc.* Sometimes, of course, the nick-name bears no relation to the original name; even today,

Nicknames (*continued*)

many people answer to nick-names that do not relate to their official names, e.g. Paddy for an Irishman, Lanky for a tall person. Such names are not necessarily complimentary!

Nobility

See Aristocracy and Nobility

Nonconformist Registers

The keeping of registers of baptisms/births, marriages and burials by the non-conformist denominations was slow to begin, since their activities were initially illegal. Hardwick's *Marriage Act 1753 prohibited marriage outside of the Church of England between 1754 and 1837; nonconformists often did not have their own burial grounds; Methodists in particular did not regard themselves as outside of the Church of England to begin with, and so used its ceremonies for baptisms, marriages and burials.

By the Non-Parochial Registers Act of 1840, the non-conformists were requested to deposit existing registers with the Registrar General. A further request was made in 1857, and some 9,000 registers were deposited. These are now in the *Public Record Office. However, not all registers were surrendered; in particular, *Roman Catholics were reluctant to hand them over. Many registers have since been deposited in county record offices and elsewhere.

Further Reading:

- *General Register Office: Registers of births, marriages and deaths, surrendered to the non-parochial registers commissions, RG4 and RG8.* 2 vols. List and Index Society **265-6.** 1996. Supersedes the Society's vol. **42.**

Nonconformists

The term 'nonconformist' was originally applied to those who refused to accept the 1662 prayer book in its entirety. Over 2,000 clergymen were ejected from their livings and formed the nucleus of the early nonconformist denominations (other than the Quakers, who had no clergy). *Presbyterians, *Congregationalist (independents) and *Baptists slowly emerged as separate denominations in the course of the later seventeeth century, although the boundaries between them were very fluid, and some churches changed the labels attached to them. After the Toleration Act, 1689, they were allowed to worship freely, provided they obtained meeting house licences; many groups abandoned their Calvinist belief and became Unitarian. Towards the end of the eighteenth century, the Wesleyan revival led to the Methodist movement, and many new churches were founded. By 1851, the non-conformist denominations, together with the *Roman Catholics, formed almost fifty per cent of the church-going population.

The records of the non-conformists are extensive, and may be found in the *Public Record Office, *county record offices, and with the churches themselves. Further details are given here under each denomination. Many sources, indexes *etc.,* relating to non-conformists are held by *Dr. Williams Library.

Further Reading:

- SHORNEY, DAVID. *Protestant nonconformity and Roman Catholicism: a guide to sources in the Public Record Office.* Readers guide **13**. P.R.O. Publications, 1996.
- MOLLETT, M. *Sources for the history of English nonconformity 1660-1830.* Archives and the user **8**. British Records Association, 1991.
- STEEL, D.J. *Sources for nonconformist genealogy and family history.* National index of parish registers, **2**. Society of Genealogists, 1973.

Non-Parochial Registers

The ceremonies of the Church of England did not always take place in parish churches. Work-houses, hospitals, colleges, schools, and a variety of other institutions all had

Non-Parochial Registers (*continued*)

chapels, and in some instances kept their own registers of births, marriages and deaths. The term also applies to the registers of overseas Anglican communities. It is sometimes also applied to non-conformist registers, but these are best considered separately - although a few non-parochial registers were surrendered to the Registrar General and are now kept with nonconformist registers in classes RG4-8.

Norman Conquest

The Norman conquest almost totally displaced the Anglo-Saxon nobility: almost all lords recorded in *Domesday Book were Normans or their allies. They all held their lands either directly or indirectly from the crown in return for military service (see *Feudalism). Theoretically, it is possible to trace descent from domesday tenants; it is doubtful, however, that anyone can prove descent from an ancestor who fought at Hastings.

Further Reading:

- CAMP, ANTHONY J. *My ancestors came with the Conqueror.* Society of Genealogists, 1990.

North America

See Canada, and United States

Notes and Queries

This journal is a medium of information exchange covering all subjects, but especially literature and history. Its contents are mostly supplied by readers in response to other readers questions, and include much genealogical information. Runs are widely available in libraries.

A number of similar journals exist or have existed devoted to the history of particular counties, e.g. *Devon and Cornwall notes and queries.* Their genealogical content is often noted in the county volumes of Raymond's *British genealogical library guides.*

Nuncupative

A nuncupative will was one made before witnesses by word of mouth; only later, after death, was it written down. The witnesses would testify to its authenticity in the relevant probate court.

Nurse Children

In former times, babies were often sent away from their families to be nursed. If they died, they were often described as 'nurse children' in parish registers.

Further Reading:

- CLARK, GILLIAN. 'London's first evacuees: a population study of nurse children', *Local historian* **19**(3), 1989, 100-106.

O

Oaths of Allegiance

In times of crisis, and as security measures, governments have at various times required its subjects to take oaths of allegiance. The best known of these is the *Protestation, ordered by Parliament at the beginning of the civil war in 1641/2. This was followed by the *Solemn League and Covenant of 1643, the *Association oath of 1696, and various others. Where they survive, the lists of those who took these oaths can provide valuable clues to the genealogist.

Obituaries

Obituaries in newspapers and magazines are valuable sources, and offer information that may not be available elsewhere, although they should be used cautiously. Those in the *Gentlemans magazine* have been indexed. Many others published prior to 1800 are indexed by Musgrave. Journals related to religion or occupations include many obituaries, as do the transactions of various learned societies - including those of county historical societies. There are, for example; many obituaries of methodists in the *Methodist magazine,* 1798-1821.

Further Reading:
• MUSGRAVE, W. *Obituary prior to 1800 (as far as it relates to England, Scotland and Ireland).* 6 vols. Harleian Society **44-9.** 1899-1901.

Occupations

The occupations in which our forefathers were engaged have left behind them masses of documentation. Personnel records such as job applications and wage lists, trade journals, membership lists of professional bodies, *trade directories, accounts, newspaper advertisements, *etc., etc.,* may all yield useful information. Occupational dictionaries, such as that by the Twinings, provide information on particular trades, and explain some of the obscurer terms for occupations no longer followed. Many *biographical dictionaries for specific occupations, e.g. librarians, furniture makers are available, as are a variety of guides to sources for e.g. gasworkers, victuallers, ship-builders, *etc.* Numerous publications on historic occupations are available and are listed by Raymond; the family historian needs to review any which bear on known occupations of his ancestors.

Web Page
- United Kingdom and Ireland Occupations
  www.genuki.org.uk/big/Occupations.html

Further Reading:
- TWINING, ANDREW, & TWINING, SANDRA. *Dictionary of old trades and occupations.* Kogarah, N.S.W.: the authors, 1993.
- RAYMOND, STUART A. *Occupational sources for genealogists.* 2nd ed. F.F.H.S., 1996. Bibliography.
- RAYMOND, STUART A. *Londoners occupations: a genealogical guide.* 2nd ed. F.F.H.S., 2001. Similar volumes are available for Surrey and Sussex, and for Yorkshire.

Official
The deputy of a bishop or archdeacon in judicial matters. He often granted probate, and his name may be written on the back of probate records.

One-Name Studies
See Guild of One-Name Studies

Oral History
Your elderly relatives may know a great deal about your family history, and may remember things they were told by their grandparents. That information could easily take you

Oral History (*continued*)

back 150 years, and provides an obvious starting place for your family history research. It may also be information not available from any other source. There is, however, a technique to interviewing relatives, and it would be advisable to consult some of the books listed below before you get your tape recorder out. You should also be aware that memory is not always accurate. Always check what you are told against documentary evidence, if at all possible.

Further Reading:

- McLAUGHLIN, E. *Interviewing elderly relatives.* 3rd ed. Haddenham: Varneys Press, 1993.
- TAYLOR, LAWRENCE. *Oral evidence and the family historian: a short guide.* F.F.H.S., 1984.
- THOMPSON, P. *The voice of the past: oral history.* Oxford University Press, 1978.
- PERKS, ROBERT. *Oral history: talking about the past.* Rev. ed. Helps for students of history **94**. Historical Association, 1995.
- CAUNCE, STEPHEN. *Oral history and the local historian.* Longman, 1994.

Ordinary

A term which has a variety of meanings. Those which are most likely to be encountered by family historians are:
i.   In the church, one who has authority; a judge.
ii.   In heraldry, a collection of coats of arms.

Ordination

The ceremony by which one becomes a clergyman.

Oriental and India Office Collections

The library of the India Office is now a part of the *British Library. Its holdings include the archives of the *East India Company, which administered India prior to the Indian mutiny of 1857. A wide variety of records are available. Particularly important are the writers petitions (i.e.

applications for jobs), which include baptismal certificates, testimonials, and details of education. In 1806, the Company established Haileybury College to train its servants, and its registers are important. Service records of the Indian Army provide details of the career of soldiers, as do the various published army lists. Records of births, marriages and deaths are also available, as are probate records, and many other sources which cannot be listed here. A variety of publications are listed under the heading 'East Indiamen', in Raymond's *Occupational sources for genealogists* 2nd ed. F.F.H.S., 1996.

Web Pages:
- India Office Records: Family History Sources
  www.bl.uk/collections/oiocfamilyhistory/family.html
  The British Library's official page.

- The India Office Records
  www.alphalink.com.au/~aigs/india.htm
  Page on the site of the Australian Institute of Genealogical Studies

Further Reading:
- MOIR, M. *A general guide to the India Office records.* British Library, 1988.
- BAXTER, I.A. *A brief guide to biographical sources.* 2nd ed. India Office Library & Records (British Library), 1990.

Orphans
The care of orphans was the responsibility of the parish, and evidence relating to them will be found in the accounts of churchwardens and overseers of the poor. They were usually apprenticed to trade or husbandry (see *apprentices). After 1834, *poor law boards of guardians often established orphanages. In the late eighteenth and nineteenth centuries, a variety of childrens' societies, e.g. the *Barnardo Homes, were established to cater for homeless children.

Out Pensioners
See Chelsea Pensioners

Overseas Research
Genealogical sources for foreign countries can be very different from those available in this country, and anyone trying to trace births, marriages and deaths overseas, needs a basic understanding of the way in which records have been kept in the country concerned. This dictionary includes brief articles on *Australia, *Canada, *France, *Germany, *India, *Ireland, *New Zealand and the *United States. The *Society of Genealogists and the *British Library, amongst others, hold many books and journals relating to research in other countries.

Evidence on deaths overseas may also be available in England. The Bishop of London was responsible for overseas churches, and therefore received many registers and bishops transcripts, now held at the *Public Record Office and the *Guildhall Library. A few overseas registers and bishops' transcripts are also held by *Lambeth Palace Library. The Registrar General held birth, marriage and death registers relating to the armed forces overseas; he also held registers kept by British consuls. Some of these are now in the keeping of the *Public Record Office. The *Oriental and India Office collection of the British Library has ecclesiastical returns of births, marriages and deaths from India, Burma and St. Helena. Monumental inscriptions in India are the focus of the British Association for Cemeteries in South Asia.

Further Reading:
• YEO, GEOFFREY. *The British Overseas: a guide to records of their baptisms, births, marriages, deaths and burials available in the United Kingdom.* 3rd ed. Guildhall Library, 1994.

Overseers
See Poor Law

P

Palaeography
See Hand-Writing

Pallots Marriage Index
This index covers almost all parishes in the City of London,
1780-1837. It also indexes many Middlesex registers, and has
been augmented by index entries from many other counties
(mostly taken from printed sources). The original index is
held by the *Institute of Heraldic and Genealogical Studies,
but it is searchable on the Ancestry.com website.

Web Page:
• Pallots Marriage Index 1780-1837
  **www.ancestry.com/search/rectype/vital/pallot/
  mainmarriage.htm**

Parish
The parish was originally an ecclesiastical area with a
church served (usually) by a single priest. Its boundaries
were those of the estate the church was founded to serve. In
some parts of the country, parishes were very large, e.g.
Leeds and Halifax in Yorkshire, and were sub-divided into
chapelries (see *Chapel/Chapelry) or townships; many of
these became parishes in the nineteenth century.

Under the Tudors, the parish became the basic
administrative unit of local government and remained so
until the nineteenth century. Its vestry appointed parish
officers - *churchwardens, *constables, overseers, waywardens
etc., - who had responsibility for petty law and order, local
taxation, relief of the poor, maintainance of the highways,
and a variety of other local government functions. This was

Parish (*continued*)

in addition to the parish's ecclesiastical functions, such as maintaining the church fabric, exercising control over the morals and beliefs of the inhabitants, administering any parochial property, *etc.* *Quarter sessions and *justices of the peace exercised supervision over civil matters - and sometimes strayed into ecclesiastical territory. In the nineteenth-century, many functions were transferred to other bodies - poor law unions, county, urban and district councils, *etc.*

The activities of parish officers are documented extensively by the records formerly stored in parish chests, and now mostly in *county record offices. See *parish records.

Further Reading:
* POUNDS, N.J.G. *A history of the English parish: the culture of religion from Augustine to Victoria.* Cambridge University Press, 2000.

Parish Records

A term frequently, but carelessly, used as a synonym for *parish registers. Parish registers are parish records, true, but so are a wide variety of other records - churchwardens accounts, *title deeds of parish property, overseers accounts, settlement certificates, *glebe terriers, rate assessments, vestry minutes, way-wardens accounts, *etc., etc.* All these documents were kept in the parish chest; most have now been deposited in county record offices.

Further Reading:
* TATE, W.E. *The parish chest: a study of the records of parochial administration in England.* 3rd ed. Phillimore, 1983.

Parish Registers

Registers of births, marriages and deaths were first ordered to be kept in England in 1538. Initially they were written on paper, often on loose sheets, and only a few registers survive from the earliest period. An order of 1597 required registers to be kept in parchment books, and instructed those reponsible to copy previous entries into that book. Consequently, most surviving registers prior to 1597 are probably not the originals, but the copies that were made at that date. The same order required transcripts of each year's register entries to be sent to the bishop; this was the origin of *bishops transcripts.

The next major change took place during the *Interregnum (1653-60), when the custody of parish registers was removed from clergymen, who also ceased to solemnize marriages. Registers during this - fortunately brief - period are badly kept if they have survived at all.

There was no standard form of entry until the middle of the eighteenth century, and the information provided in registers varies considerably from parish to parish. Often only the barest detail is given, i.e. names and dates, but sometimes occupations and places of residence are given. The information required was standardised by Lord Hardwicke's *Marriage Act 1753, and by Rose's Act 1813. Hardwicke's act required separate printed books for marriages and *banns; both parties had to sign the register, as did witnesses. Rose's act extended the requirement for a printed form to baptisms and burials. Baptismal entries were to include the names, residences and occupations or status of the parents, with the name of the officiating clergyman. Burial entries required the deceased's name, age, abode and date of burial.

Most parish registers have now been deposited in *county record offices, who can usually provide handlists of their collection (sometimes via the *internet). The *National index of parish registers* provides, county by county, a much more detailed listing. Many registers have been printed or, more recently, published on fiche; many *CD's of registers published long ago are also available (although very few

Parish Registers (*continued*)

reproduce the original registers). A number of societies have been solely concerned with publishing parish registers: the national Parish Register Society's activities in the early part of the twentieth century have been complemented by the work of county parish register societies in many counties: those for Yorkshire, Staffordshire and Lancashire have been particularly prolific, as was the register section of the Harleian Society, which concentrated primarily on London.

Many *family history societies have transcribed and indexed parish registers; some of these remain unpublished, but can be found in the relevant society's library, and perhaps in the *local studies library and / or the *Society of Genealogists. Most, however, are available on fiche or as books. A full listing of all published registers is provided in the county volumes of Raymond's *British genealogical library guides.*

Websites containing transcripts and indexes of registers are also proliferating, so much so, that Raymond requires two volumes to list them all.

Numerous indexes to parish registers have been compiled, including the massive *International genealogical index;* see *burial indexes and *marriage indexes for details.

Web Pages:

- English Parish Registers
  freepages.genealogy.rootsweb.com/~engregisters/

- Parish Register Copies in the Library of the Society of Genealogists
  www.sog.org.uk/prc/

Further Reading:

- GIBBENS, LILIAN. *Church registers.* An introduction to ... series. F.F.H.S., 1994
- PICKFORD, CHRISTOPHER J. 'Parish registers', in THOMPSON, K.M., ed. *Short guides to records. Second series guides, 25-48.* Historical Association, 1997, 33-7.

- COX, J. CHARLES. *The parish registers of England.* Methuen & Co., 1910.
- *National index of parish registers.* Society of Genealogists, 1973- . Many general and county volumes.
- HUMPHERY-SMITH, CECIL R. *Phillimore atlas and index of parish registers.* 2nd ed. Phillimore, 1994.
- RAYMOND, STUART A. *Births, marriages and deaths on the web.* 2 vols. F.F.H.S., 2002.
- *Parish register copies in the library of the Society of Genealogists.* 11th ed. Society of Genealogists, 1995.
- *Using birth, marriage and death records.* Pocket guides to family history. Public Record Office, 2000.

Parliamentary Papers

It is not generally appreciated that the sessional papers of the House of Commons form one of the most extensive series of documents ever published. They include many thousand reports from Parliamentary select committees, royal commissions, government departments, quangos, *etc.* Many of these reports contain a great deal of information likely to be of interest to local and family historians. Of particular interest are the myriad examinations of witnesses, which may throw a great deal of light on the career and character of ancestors. Many reports also include lists of names, e.g. of civil servants, paupers, victims of mining disasters, *etc., etc.* An obvious example is the *Return of owners of land 1873.*

Unfortunately, the means for identifying particular papers likely to contain lists of names or other information of relevance to genealogists is not very good. There are many guides to them, but they are not designed for genealogical purposes. The best introduction to them for the family historian is probably Powell's book.

The Parliamentary papers are widely available in reference libraries throughout the U.K., and elsewhere in the English-speaking world.

Further Reading:
- POWELL, W.R. *Local history from blue books: a select list of the sessional papers of the House of Commons.* Helps for students of history **64**. Historical Association, 1969.
- WALKER, R. S. 'Dead men do talk. Part 1. Family history sources in Parliamentary papers', *Family tree magazine* 4(6), 1988.

Parliamentary Records
See House of Lords Record Office

Parts
Lincolnshire is divided into three 'parts' - the Parts of Holland, Lindsey, and of Kesteven. The Parts of Lindsey are also divided into three *ridings.

Partible Inheritance
The systems of inheritance under which all children, or at least all sons, receive a portion of the estate of their father, in contrast to the systems of primogeniture, which were the English norm. *Gavelkind was the Kentish version of this custom.

Passenger Lists
Ships' passenger lists record the international movement of our ancestors overseas, and are useful for tracing *emigration and emigrants; they may also be worth checking for *immigrants and aliens. Not many lists survive prior to 1800. Most of those that do - with some more recent lists - have been published and are listed by Filby & Meyer.

The major British collection is that of the Board of Trade, covering 1890-1960 (in the *Public Record Office, class BT27). Its lists were required by act of Parliament, and give the names of all passengers leaving the U.K. for ports outside the Europe and the Mediterranean.

Many passenger lists are held in overseas repositories. Over 22,000,000 passengers who passed through American emigration at Ellis Island are listed on its web-site. Over 4,000 passenger lists have been transcribed by the Immigrant Ship Transcribers Guild. Many other lists are available on the web-sites identified on Hugh Reekie's site and elsewhere.

Web Sites:
- Ships Passenger Lists 1878-1960
  catalogue.pro.gov.uk/Leaflets/ri2163.htm

- Immigrant Ships Transcribers Guild
  istg.rootsweb.com

- Ships Passenger Lists: Hugh Reekie's Index of Indexes
  members.attcanada.ca/~max-com/Ships.html

- American Family Immigration History Centre ... Ellis Island
  www.ellisisland.org/

Further Reading:
- KERSHAW, ROGER. *Emigrants and expats: a guide to sources on UK emigration and residents overseas.* Public Record Office readers guide **20**. 2002.
- FILBY, P.W., & MEYER, M.K. *Passenger and immigration lists index: a guide to published arrival records of about 500,000 passengers who came to the United States and Canada in the 17th, 18th and 19th centuries.* 3 vols. Detroit: Gale, 1981. Continued by annual supplements. The works listed are indexed in: FILBY, P.W. *Passenger and immigration lists bibliography 1538-1900, being a guide to published lists of arrivals in the United State and Canada.* 2nd ed. Detroit: Gale, 1988.

Passports

Passports were not compulsory prior to 1915, although they were issued; such records as survive are fairly scanty. The *Public Record Office has passport registers 1795-1948 (FO610), and indexes of applicants 1851-62 and 1874-1916 (FO611); these mainly give names and dates, although earlier

Passports (*continued*)

registers also give destinations. For the seventeenth century there are some registers of 'licences to pass beyond the seas' in E157; amongst the State papers there are entry books of passes for 1650-60 (SP25/111-6) and 1674-1784 (SP44/334-413); a further entry book for 1748-94 is at FO366/544.

Web Page:
- Passport Records
  www.pro.gov.uk/leaflets/ri2167.htm

Patent Rolls

Letters patent were used to make crown grants and confirmations of land, privileges, *licences, *denization, liberties, wardships, *etc.,* to both individuals and institutions. They are recorded in the patent rolls, which run from 1201 to 1946, and are in the *Public Record Office (C66).

Further Reading:
- *Patent rolls of the reign of Henry III ... A.D. 1216-1225.* H.M.S.O., 1901. Many further volumes continue the series to 1582.

Peculiars

A 'peculiar' was an area outside of ordinary ecclesiastical jurisdiction; most had probate jurisdiction, and some issued marriage licences. A peculiar might be a parish, a manor or a liberty; jurisdiction might be exercised by the bishop of another diocese, by the dean and chapter of a cathedral, by a manorial lord, by the crown, or by a variety of other people. The parish of Uffculme, for example, was within the diocese of Exeter, but was a peculiar of the diocese of Salisbury. Consequently, its probate records escaped the destruction which engulfed most Devon wills when the Exeter probate registry was bombed in the second world war. The probate records of the manor of Cockington, which was a manorial peculiar, also survived, as did those of the Exeter orphans court.

When searching for probate records, it is necessary to be aware that there may have been peculiars in the area being searched. Peculiars are mapped in:

- HUMPHERY-SMITH, CECIL R., ed. *Phillimores atlas and index of parish registers.* 2nd ed. Phillimore, 1995.

Pedigrees

A pedigree is a chart showing the descent of a particular family, and is the end-result of strictly genealogical (rather than family history) research. Genealogists have constructed innumerable pedigrees; for information on finding them, see *Family Histories and Pedigrees. There are a variety of ways in which they can be drawn; detailed guidance is given in:

- LYNSKEY, MARIE. *Family trees: a manual for their design,layout & display.* Phillimore, 1996.

Peerage

Peers are members of the House of Lords. Until the twentieth century, and with the exception of the bishops and law lords, their rank was hereditary. A variety of works on their pedigrees are listed in Raymond's *English genealogy: a bibliography.* 3rd ed. F.F.H.S., 1996.

Further Reading:

- C[OKAYNE], G.E. *The complete peerage of England, Scotland, Ireland, Great Britain and the United Kingdom, extant or dormant.* New ed. 13 vols in 6. Gloucester: Sutton, 1981. Originally published 1910-59.
- *Burke's peerage and baronetage.* 2 vols. 106th ed. Burkes Peerage (Genealogical Books), 1999.

Periodicals

There are numerous periodicals of value to family historians. *Family tree magazine* is a commercial production; the *Society of Genealogists issues the *Genealogists' magazine,* and the *Federation of Family History Societies has its *Family history news and digest.* These are the best known

Periodicals (*continued*)

titles, and all are worth reading regularly. Virtually all
*family history societies issue their own journals or
newsletters; these usually include details of current
activities, members' *interests lists, and articles of general
interest, or reporting research on particular families. The
'digest' section of *Family history news and digest* provides
regular indexing of the articles in these journals.

It is still worth checking the back-runs of genealogical
journals published in the nineteenth and early twentieth
centuries. These contain numerous family histories,
pedigrees, and transcripts of sources; their contents are
listed in:

• RAYMOND, STUART. *British genealogical periodicals: a
  bibliography of their contents.* 3 vols. in 5. F.F.H.S., 1991-3.

Family and local historians have many interests in
common, and the transactions and journals of local and
county historical or archaeological societies frequently
contain articles of interest to both. Don't be put off by the
word 'archaeological': its usage has changed since the
nineteenth century, when it was frequently intended to
include genealogy.

Most of these societies have published detailed indexes of
contents, which are worth checking. Relevant articles are
listed in the county volumes of Raymond's *British
genealogical library guides* and in various other
bibliographies.

Further Reading:

• CHAPMAN, COLIN. *An introduction to using newspapers
  and periodicals.* F.F.H.S., 1996.

Phillimore Parish Register Series

This series provides published transcripts of some 1,400
marriage registers from many counties. Many of its volumes
are now available on CD. Although it is a widely used series,

the words of warning below (see *transcripts) applies with force to this series: the Phillimore transcript for Week St. Mary, Cornwall, must take the prize for the most mis-leading transcript ever published. Almost half of the entries are incorrect! Phillimore recruited many transcribers country-wide for his project, but in this instance he made a poor choice.

Further Reading:

- *Phillimore's parish register series (marriage).* 240 vols. Phillimore, 1896-1938.
- BRYANT-ROSIER, M. *Index to parishes in Phillimore's marriages.* Family Tree Magazine, 1988.

Photographs

Photography was a nineteenth-century invention, although to begin with it was a fairly expensive process. Consequently, family photographs were often taken by a professional, rather than a family member. Innumerable studio photographs survive; if any have come down to you they may add considerably to the interest of your family history. Unfortunately many old photographs do not include the names of the persons portrayed - hence it may help if they can be dated. Several books offer help with this process.

Photographs may also be available showing scenes from your ancestors lives - the house they lived in, the church where they were married, their business premises. *Local studies libraries often have photographic collections relating to their own localities. There is also something to be said for taking your own photographs of such localities. Postcards may also be useful, both for topographical scenes, and also for portraits.

Further Reading:

- POLS, ROBERT. *Understanding old photographs.* Witney: Robert Boyd Publications, 1995.
- POLS, ROBERT. *Family photographs 1860-1945.* Public Record Office, 2002.

- POLS, ROBERT. *Photography for family historians.* F.F.H.S., 1998.
- STEEL, DON, & TAYLOR, LAWRENCE. *Family history in focus.* Lutterworth Press, 1984.

Pipe Rolls

Pipe rolls are the annual accounts of the sheriffs as sent to the Court of Exchequer. They run from the twelfth to the nineteenth centuries, and are in the *Public Record Office, class E372. Many of the earliest rolls have been published by the Pipe Roll Society, and are listed in *Texts and calendars.* They record many names, and allow the succession of tenants in chief to be traced.

Further Reading:

- CROOK, DAVID. 'Pipe rolls', in THOMPSON, K.M., ed. *Short guides to records. Second series, guides 25-48.* Historical Association, 1997, 75-82.

Place-Names

Place-names are an interesting study in themselves, but most genealogists will primarily be interested in using them to locate their ancestors. The entries on *maps and *gazetteers suggest some ways of doing this.

It might also be noted that some surnames are derived from place-names, and may suggest where your ancestors came from. It is, of course, also possible that a place name may derive from a surname.

Plea Rolls

Plea rolls record actions brought under the common law, and are found amongst the archives of the Curia Regis and its successors - the *courts of Kings Bench, Common Pleas, Exchequer, *etc.* in the *Public Record Office, running from the reign of Richard I to 1873. Many early rolls have been published, especially by the Selden Society; full details are given in * *Texts and calendars.*

Poll Books

Poll books record the names of voters in Parliamentary, and, occasionally, other elections, together with their votes. There is no consistency in the information given, or in the arrangement of the volumes. The latter may be alphabetical, by parish or by ward, but it may also be in the order in which votes were taken! Sometimes occupations and qualifications are given, indicating the basis on which they were entitled to vote (see *Franchise).

Poll books can list many thousand names, and enable the family historian to trace the distribution of surnames across entire counties. Many survive; the best collections are at the Institute for Historical Research, Guildhall Library, and the *British Library. They may also be found in most county record offices and local studies libraries. A few have been reprinted in recent years, mainly by the present author.

Web Pages:
- Raymond's Original Pollbooks
  www.samjraymond.btinternet.co.uk/pb2.html

Further Reading:
- GIBSON, JEREMY, & ROGERS, COLIN. *Poll books c.1696-1872: a directory to holdings in Great Britian.* 2nd ed. F.F.H.S., 1990.
- SIMS, J. *A handlist of British parliamentary poll books.* University of Leicester History Dept. occasional publications **4**. 1984.
- *Poll-books of Nottingham and Nottinghamshire, 1710.* Thoroton Society record series **18**. 1958.
- CANNON, JOHN. 'Poll books', in MUNBY, L.M. ed. *Short guides to records. First series, guides 1-24.* [Rev.ed.] Historical Association, 1994, 25-8.

Poll Tax

Poll taxes are a tax on heads, and as such have proved very unpopular - causing the Peasants revolt of 1381, and

Poll Tax (*continued*)

assisting the demise of Margaret Thatcher in 1990. For family historians, however, the records of poll taxes, although fragmentary, can be useful. Names from the assessments of 1379, 1380 and 1381 have been published in full. The tax was levied again in 1641, and on eight occasions between 1660 and 1697. Such returns as survive are in the Public Record Office (E179), and have been listed by Gibson, *et al.* Those fragments which have been published are listed in the county volumes of Raymond's *British genealogical library guides.*

Further Reading:

- FENWICK, CAROLYN C., ed. *The poll taxes 1377, 1379 and 1381.* 2 vols. Records of social and economic history **27** & **29.** Oxford University Press for the British Academy, 1998-2000. A third volume is forthcoming.
- GIBSON, JEREMY, & DELL, ALAN. *The protestation returns 1641-42 and other contemporary listings.* F.F.H.S. 1995. Includes listings of poll tax assessments 1641.
- GIBSON, J.S.W. *The hearth tax, other late Stuart tax lists, and the Association Oath rolls.* 2nd ed. F.F.H.S., 1996. Includes listing of poll tax assessments for 1660, 1667, 1678, 1689, 1691, 1694 and 1697.
- LAWTON, G.O. ed. *Northwich Hundred poll tax 1660 and hearth tax 1664.* Record Society of Lancashire and Cheshire **119.** 1979.

Poor Law

'The poor will be always with you.' The words of Jesus (Matthew 26, v.11) have been true throughout English history, and the efforts which have gone into dealing with the problem have resulted in a huge quantity of documentation, of great value to family historians.

Two dates define the history of poor relief. In 1597, the Poor Law Act required parishes to relieve their own poor, created the office of overseer, and authorized the levying of poor rates. In 1834, the New Poor Law Act removed responsibility from the parish to the 'Union' of parishes, creating elected Boards of Guardians to undertake responsibility for each Union.

The eligibility of paupers for relief was from 1662 dependent on their place of settlement. *Parishes, and, later, Unions, were only required to relieve those paupers whose settlement was in their own area. Furthermore, anyone settling in a parish could be removed to his / her place of settlement if it was 'considered likely' that he or she would become 'chargeable' to the parish. Consequently, Justices of the Peace were required to determine the settlement of both those claiming relief, and those who might claim it. The resultant settlement examinations provide mini-biographies of the poor, detailing their birth-place and their wanderings. If, as a consequence of their examination, the J.P.s decided to remove an examinee, they issued a removal order, which gave brief details of how settlement had been gained in the receiving parish.

In order to avoid the possibility of removal, it was desirable to obtain a settlement certificate from the parish of settlement acknowledging their responsibility to give relief in case of need. Needless to say, parishes were anxious to avoid needless expense and consequently, there were frequent disputes in *Quarter Sessions between parishes concerning the settlement of particular paupers. Quarter sessions records also include much information on matters such as vagrancy and *illegitimacy, both major charges on the poor rate. Assessment of rates was a matter for the parish itself, and details are likely to be in the overseers accounts, with the parish records.

The law of settlement continued to apply after 1834; however, documentation will be with Union rather than parish records; these are in *county record offices. Gibson *et al* take no less than four pages to list the various types of records available - accounts, admission books, registers of

Poor Law (*continued*)

inmates, rate books, *etc., etc.* The principle of 'less eligibility' underlay the new act; this meant that paupers had to be poorer than the poorest person in work, and required them (in theory) to accept relief in the Union's workhouse. The Unions were closely supervised by the central Poor Law Board in order to ensure that the law was strictly applied; its extensive records are in the *Public Record Office.

Further Reading:

- COLE, ANNE. *Poor Law documents before 1834.* 2nd ed. F.F.H.S., 2000.
- McLAUGHLIN, EVE. *Annals of the poor.* 5th ed. Haddenham: Varneys Press, 1994.
- OXLEY, G. W. 'Overseers accounts', in THOMPSON, K.M. *hort guides to records. Second series, guides 25-48.* Historical Associations, 1997,pp.21-4.
- THOMPSON, K.M. 'Settlement papers', in: THOMPSON, K.M. *hort guides to records. Second series, guides 25-48.* Historical Associations, 1997, pp.25-8.
- REID, ANDY. *The Union workhouse: a study guide for teachers and local historians.* Learning local history **3**. Phillimore for the British Association for Local History, 1994.
- GIBSON, JEREMY, *et al. Poor law union records.* 2nd ed. 4 vols. F.F.H.S., 1997-2000.
- HITCHCOCK, TIM, & BLACK, JOHN. eds. *Chelsea settlement and bastardy examinations, 1733-1766.* London Record Society **33**. 1999.
- PILBEAM, NORMA, & NELSON, IAN, eds. *Poor law records of mid-Sussex 1601-1835.* Sussex Record Society **83**. 1999.
- SLACK, PAUL, ed. *Poverty in early Stuart Salisbury.* Wiltshire Record Society **31**. 1975.
- POUND, JOHN F. ed. *The Norwich census of the poor, 1570.* Norfolk Record Society **40**. 1971.
- SOKOLL, THOMAS. ed. *Essex pauper letters 1731-1837.* Records of social and economic history. New series **30**. 2001.

Portraits

Portraits of ancestors are invaluable, but not frequently found by family historians (unless they are *photographs or *postcards). Many portraits exist in both public and private art collections; an extensive listing of the portraits of famous people, indicating their whereabouts, is provided by Ormond & Rogers. If you have a portrait which could be of one of your ancestors, it should be possible to date it roughly from the evidence of costume and hairstyle; art historians may be able to identify the painter and perhaps provide more information; ask at your local art gallery, or contact the National Portrait Gallery's Heinz Archive and Library at St. Martin's Place, London, WC2H 0HE.

Web Page:
- National Portrait Gallery
  www.npg.org.uk

Further Reading:
- ORMOND, RICHARD, & ROGERS, MALCOLM, ed. *Dictionary of British portraiture*. 4 vols. B.T. Batsford, in association with the National Portrait Gallery, 1979-81.

Postcards

Postcards, which were first used for postal purposes in 1894, can be valuable sources of information for genealogists. If you - or another relative - is lucky enough to have inherited postcards sent to an ancestor, the messages and addresses on them are worthy of close examination. The photographs on them may be of help too - many portraits, especially of clergymen and entertainers, were issued as post-cards. Topographical postcards may also embellish your family history if they show the villages in which ancestors lived, their church, or even their house.

Postcard collecting is now a popular hobby, and there are many dealers in the field, some of whom attend family history fairs. Postcard fairs are regularly held in many places, and are worth attending.

Web Site:
- Postcard Pages
  www.postcard.co.uk

Further Reading:
- GODDEN, GEOFFREY A. *Collecting picture postcards.*
  Phillimore, 1996.

Prerogative Court of Canterbury

The P.C.C. was, until 1858, the highest probate court in England, and was entitled to prove the wills of those who had property in more than one diocese. It could also be used by anyone seeking to prove a will in the Province of Canterbury, and in practise many executors of wealthy testators proved *wills in the Prerogative court, rather than in diocesan or archdeaconry courts, whether on grounds of prestige or greater security. Between 1653 and 1660, it was the only probate court in operation.

There are published indexes to P.C.C. wills for 1383-1700 and 1750-1800, to administration bonds 1559-1660, and to some *probate inventories (not many survive). A number of volumes provide full abstracts of wills. A full listing of published resources is given in Raymond's *English genealogy: a bibliography.* 3rd ed. F.F.H.S., 1996, and also in Scott. The latter also includes details of unpublished indexes. An index to P.C.C. wills 1750-1800 is available on the English Origins website.

Web Pages:
- How to use P.C.C. wills before 1700
  www.pro.gov.uk/research/leaflets/willsbefore.htm

- How to use P.C.C. wills after 1700
  www.pro.gov.uk/research/leaflets/willsafter.htm

- How to use P.C.C. administrations before 1700
  www.pro.gov.uk/research/leaflets/admin1.htm

- How to use P.C.C. administrations after 1700
  www.pro.gov.uk/research/leaflets/admin2.htm

- Prerogative Court of Canterbury Wills Index 1750-1800
  www.englishorigins.com/help/pccwills-details.aspx

Further Reading:
- SCOTT, MARIAM. *Prerogative Court of Canterbury: Wills and other probate records.* Public Record Office readers guide, **15**. 1997.

Prerogative Court of York

The P.C.Y. had similar jurisdiction to that of the Prerogative Court of Canterbury in the Northern Province, i.e. the Archdiocese of York. Its records are held at the *Borthwick Institute of Historical Research. Indexes 1589-1688 have been published in 15 volumes of the Yorkshire Archaeological Society's record series.

Presbyterians

The Presbyterians were the largest group of dissenters from the Restoration settlement of 1660, although by the nineteenth century they had become one of the smaller denominations; many of their churches had become *Unitarian. Originally, there was little to differentiate than from the *Congregationalists; they dissented from the established church on the question of church government. Many of their registers are now with other *nonconformist registers in the *Public Record Office. Details of these and other records for each church are given in:
- RUSTON. ALAN. *My ancestors were English Presbyterians or Unitarians: how can I find out more about them?* 2nd ed. Society of Genealogists, 2001.
- 'The three denominations: the Presbyterians (including Unitarians), Independents (or Congregationalists) and Baptists', in STEEL. D.J. *Sources for nonconformist genealogy and family history.* National index of parish registers, **2**. Society of Genealogists, 1973, 519-600.

Presentments

Presentments were made by *churchwardens at ecclesiastical visitations. They are reports of mis-demeanours committed within their parish. Presentments could also be made by jurors and other officers in a variety of courts.

Primary Sources

The primary sources for the family historian will usually be documentary in character, although *oral history may also be of importance. You do need to be able to evaluate your primary sources. Questions you might ask of them include the following:

1. Is the source authentic? Is it what it purports to be?
2. What was the origin of the source?
3. When was it produced?
4. Why was it produced?
5. Do you understand its meaning?
6. Can you place the information it contains into the context of what you already know? Does the information fit?

Printed books, generally, are not primary sources, although they may re-produce primary sources. If at all possible, you should always check evidence that has been published against the original manuscript.

Primogeniture

Primogeniture was the most usual inheritance custom in England. Under it, the eldest son inherited the landed property of his father.

Prisoners

See Convicts and Prisoners

Prisoners of War and Civilian Internees

There is no single source for tracing prisoners of war. A variety of records relating to wars from the late eighteenth century onwards are held by the *Public Record Office. The

*Imperial War Museum also holds some information. For the Second World War, the International Council of the Red Cross, Archives Division, 19 Avenue de la Paix, CH - 1202, Geneva, Switzerland, holds an incomplete listing of P.o.W's and internees of all nationalities, which can only by consulted by post.

Web Pages:

- British Prisoners of War, c.1760-1919
  catalogue.pro.gov.uk/Leaflets/ri2012.htm
- Prisoners of War, British 1939-1953
  catalogue.pro.gov.uk/Leaflets/ri2020.htm

Further Reading:

- KERSHAW, ROGER. *Emigrants and expats: a guide to sources on UK emigration and residents overseas.* Public Record Office readers guide **20.** 2002. (Chapter 6 deals with PoWs).
- *List of British officers taken prisoner in the various theatres of war between August 1914 and November 1918.* Cox & Co., 1919.

Probate Accounts

Executors and administrators were required to submit accounts of how they had disposed of the goods belonging to the deceased. These accounts do not survive in large numbers; however, where they do they may prove useful to the genealogist. They name the executor(s) or administrator(s), showing the relationship(s) to the deceased. They show the listed value of the estate as recorded in the *probate inventory, any costs incurred in administering the estate, and the names of all persons to whom payments had been made, both legatees and creditors.

Not all collections of probate accounts have been indexed. Sometimes they are filed with other *probate records, sometimes separately. An extensive, but incomplete, index is provided by Spufford, who also provides a detailed introduction.

Further Reading:
- SPUFFORD, PETER, ed. *Index to the probate accounts of England and Wales.* 2 vols. Index Library **112-3.** 1999.
- BOWER, JACQUELINE. 'Probate accounts' in THOMPSON, K.M., ed. *Short guides to records. Second series, guides 25-48.* Historical Association, 1997, 55-8.

Probate Inventories

Probate inventories list the goods owned by deceased individuals. They were compiled by two or more neighbours, who are named, and value all moveable property - furniture, clothing, utensils, crops, livestock, tools, trade goods, debts owed to the deceased, *etc.* They do not, however, include real estate (other than leasehold property).

Inventories were kept with other *probate records, sometimes filed with wills, sometimes separately. With the exception of *Prerogative Court of Canterbury inventories, they can now mostly be found in *county record offices. Many have been published by *record societies and others; comprehensive listings of such publications are given in the county volumes of Raymond's *British genealogical library guides.*

Further Reading:
- STEER, F.W. 'Probate inventories', in MUNBY, L.M., ed. *Short guides to records. First series, 1-24.* [Rev. ed.] Historical Association, 1994, 29-32.
- COX, NANCY, & COX, JEFF. 'Probate inventories: the legal background', *Local historian* **16,** 1984, 133-45 & 217-27.
- STEER, F.W., ed. *Farm and cottage inventories of mid-Essex 1635-1749.* 2nd ed. Phillimore, 1969.
- TRINDER, BARRIE, COX, JEFF, eds. *Yeomen and colliers in Telford: Probate inventories for Dawley, Lilleshall, Wellington and Wrockwardine, 1660-1750.* Phillimore, 1980.

Probate Records

The process of probate produced a huge mass of documentation, which is to be found in numerous record offices throughout the country. It began with the writing of the will or the grant of letters of administration (see *administration bonds), continued with the compilation of a *probate inventory, may have involved various legal proceedings, and ended (theoretically) with the compilation of the executor's or administrator's accounts. The information provided is extensive; where probate records survive they are vital sources for family historians.

Numerous probate courts were active in England and Wales, hence the wide distribution of records. Until 1858, jurisdiction was exercised mainly by ecclesiastical courts. Most archdeacons had testamentary jurisdiction. If a testator had property in two archdeaconries, his will had to be proved in the bishop's consistory or commissary court; if he had property in two dioceses, then it had to be proved in one of the prerogative courts. The *wills of persons of substance were often proved in a higher court, in order to take advantage of its authority, and for reasons of prestige. Wills could also be proved in some peculiar courts - including a handful which were not ecclesiastical. During the Commonwealth (1653-1660) all wills were proved in the Prerogative Court of Canterbury.

Most pre-1858 probate records have been indexed, and most indexes have been published. The *Index library* includes numerous indexes to probate records; details of these and some other published indexes are given in *Texts and calendars.* A full listing of pre-1858 probate courts, their records, and indexes, is given by Gibson and Churchill. *Death duty registers may enable you to locate the court in which a will was proved, and thus act as a central location index. There have been many published editions of probate records; these, together with comprehensive listings of indexes, and other probate-related publications, are listed in

Probate Records (*continued*)

the county volumes of Raymond's *British genealogical library guides;* those published by *record societies are listed in *Texts and calendars.*

Since 1858, all probate jurisdiction has been exercised by the Probate Division (now Family Division) of the High Court; copies of all wills and letters of administration are held at the Principal Registry of the Family Division, Probate Department, First Avenue House, 42-9, High Holborn, London WC1V 6NP. A full index is available; indexes and copy wills may sometimes also be consulted locally.

Web Pages:

- Wills and Death Duty Records after 1858
  catalogue.pro.gov.uk/leaflets/ri2301.htm

- Probate Records
  catalogue.pro.gov.uk/leaflets/ri2241.htm

- Wills before 1858: Where to Start
  catalogue.pro.gov.uk/leaflets/ri2302.htm

- Probate Records from 1858
  www.pro.gov.uk/research/leaflets/probatefrom1858.htm

Further Reading:

- GIBSON, JEREMY, & CHURCHILL, ELSE. *Probate jurisdictions: where to look for wills.* 5th ed. F.F.H.S., 2002.
- COX, J. *Affection defying the power of death: wills, probate and death duty register.* An introduction to ... series. F.F.H.S., 1993.
- ARKELL, TOM., EVANS, NESTA, & GOOSE, NIGEL, eds. *When death us do part: understanding and interpreting the probate records of early modern England.* Oxford: Leopards Head Press, 2000.
- NEWINGTON-IRVINE, NICHOLAS. *Will indexes and other probate material in the library of the Society of Genealogists.* Society of Genealogists, 1996.

- BRINKWORTH, E.R.C., & GIBSON, J.S.W., eds. *Banbury wills and inventories.* 2 vols. Banbury Historical Society 13-14. 1976-85.
- BERRY, ELIZABETH K., ed. *Swaledale wills and inventories 1522-1600.* Yorkshire Archaeological Society record series 152. 1998.

Professional Genealogists

There is no reason why the average person cannot research his or her own family history; for many, the excitement of the chase is a major part of the reason for undertaking the task. Nevertheless, it has to be recognized that it does take time, that you may need advice, that you might not have particular skills that are needed, e.g. a knowledge of *Latin, and that you may live thousands of miles from the *record offices which hold the *archives you need to consult. These are all good reasons for seeking the help of a professional.

Professional genealogists can easily be found by consulting advertisements in genealogical magazines or on the web. However, if you want to be sure that the person you employ is properly qualified you should make sure that he / she is a member of the *Association of Genealogists and Researchers in Archives.

Further Reading:
- Employing a Professional Researcher: a practical guide **www.sog.org.uk/researcher.html**

Protestants

Protestants are Christians who reject the authority of the Pope, and believe that salvation is by faith alone, not works. The Church of England is a protestant church, and so are the nonconformist denominations.

Protestation

The protestation of 1641-2 was an oath of loyalty, ostensibly to the king, but in fact to Parliament, which all adult males

Protestation (*continued*)

(and a very few women) were required to take. Their signatures or marks are recorded, parish by parish, on the returns now in the *House of Lords Record Office.

Many returns have not survived, and coverage is now patchy. A substantial proportion of surviving returns have been published (see Gibson & Dell for details). Where returns for a whole county are available, they enable the genealogist to track the distribution of particular surnames over a wide area.

Further Reading:

- GIBSON, JEREMY. & DELL, ALAN. *The protestation returns 1641-42, and other contemporary listings.* F.F.H.S., 1995.
- GIBSON, JEREMY. ed. *Oxfordshire and North Berkshire protestation returns and tax assessments 1641-42.* 2nd ed. Oxfordshire Record Society **59**. 1994.
- RICE, R. GARRAWAY, ed. *West Sussex protestation returns 1641-2.* Sussex Record Society **5**. 1905.

Province

The dioceses under the authority of an archbishop. There were two provinces in England - Canterbury and York.

Public Libraries

See Libraries

Public Record Office

The Public Record Office, Ruskin Avenue, Kew, Richmond, Surrey, TW9 4DU, houses the extensive archives of British central government. It does not hold the national archives of Scotland and Northern Ireland, or, to a lesser extent, Wales; these countries have their own repositories. Nor does it have the archives of local government: that is the responsibility of *county record offices.

The Public Record Office at Kew is not normally the port of first call for genealogists, but it does hold a huge amount of information likely to be of interest as you pursue your research. Most people, for example, are likely to have ancestors who served in the armed forces. Most of our ancestors paid taxes. Some were criminals or bankrupts; some were transported to North America or Australia. Others were immigrants who sought *denization or *naturalization. Litigants in the central courts, diplomats, civil servants, members of the Metropolitan Police Force, merchant seaman - all may be found mentioned in Public Record Office archives. Some of the more important archives for family historians - including the *census and *Prerogative Court of Canterbury *wills - have been transferred to the *Family Records Centre.

Many Public Record Office sources are described elsewhere in this dictionary. Leaflets providing full discussions of particular sources, and instructions for searching, are available at Kew, or on the web-site. The PROCAT website provides a detailed listing of all the classes of documents held. Each document is given a reference consisting of a letter code for the court or department which created it, e.g. C for the Court of Chancery, and a number for the series, e.g. C1 is Early Chancery proceedings. This is followed by the piece number. Each 'piece' may also have internal numbering e.g. for individual pages, membranes, *etc.* This is a very simplified description; more detail is given on the web-site.

PROCAT does not as yet contain full listings of each series. For that, recourse must be had to the many typescript and manuscript lists and indexes held at Kew. Some of the most important of these have been published, either by the P.R.O. itself, or by the *List and index society.* Many P.R.O. documents have been published by record societies; these are listed in * *Texts and calendars.*

The Public Record Office was merged with the *Historical Manuscript Commission to form a new National Archives body on 1st April 2003.

Web Pages:
- Public Record Office
  www.pro.gov.uk

- An overview of the Public Record Office Website
  www.genuki.org.uk/indexes/PROcontents.html

- Public Record Office leaflets
  www.pro.gov.uk/leaflets/Riindex.asp

- Welcome to PROCAT: Public Record Office Online Catalogue
  catalogue.pro.gov.uk

Further Reading:

- BEVAN, AMANDA. *Tracing your ancestors in the Public Record Office.* 5th ed. Public Record Office handbook **19**. 2002.
- COX, JANE. *New to Kew? A first time guide for family historians at the Public Record Office, Kew.* Public Record Office readers guide **16**. 1997.
- COLWELL, STELLA. *Dictionary of genealogical sources in the Public Record Office.* Weidenfeld and Nicolson, 1992.
- COLWELL, STELLA. *Family roots: discovering the past in the Public Record Office.* Weidenfeld and Nicolson, 1991.

Q

Quakers
See Society of Friends

Quarter Days
The year was divided by custom into four quarters, marked by the quarter-days. On these days most tenancies began and ended, and rents fell due. The four days were Lady Day (March 25), Midsummer Day (June 24), Michaelmas (September 29), and Christmas (December 25).

Quarter Sessions
*Justices of the Peace met regularly at Quarter Sessions in order to judge suits and administer their counties. They heard criminal suits, supervised the poor law, the administration of *taxation, the upkeep of highways, local defence, and the county gaol, enforced the laws against *Roman Catholics, licensed traders such as victuallers and badgers, regulated wages, heard the taking of oaths, supervised the relationships between *apprentices and masters, and undertook a wide range of other tasks. Their work load increased considerably in the sixteenth and seventeenth centuries, and supplanted the role of the sheriff - although the latter presided over their meetings.

The records of Quarter Sessions were kept by the *custos rotulorum,* or clerk of the peace. They are extensive, and are the *raison d'etre* of *county record offices, forming the basis of their collections. They may be divided into five categories:
• Sessions rolls and files, being the documents actually used in court, and including lists of those present, (including J.Ps., bailiffs, jurors, high constables, prisoners, etc.), writs, presentments, indictments, depositions, petitions, licences, removal orders, sacrament certificates; also sessions books,

Quarter Sessions (*continued*)

i.e. the rough minutes of proceedings, and process books, which record names *etc.* of those indicted, details of their offences, and the court's verdict.

- Order books - the formal record of proceedings.
- Accounts of the 'county stock' shewing receipts from various levies and moneys expended. There may also be accounts of special funds such as maimed soldiers, bridges, *etc.*
- Administrative records relating to, e.g. bridges, buildings, highways, lunacy, licensing, prisons and police.
- Deposited records, including enrolled deeds, charity reports, lists of freemasons, gamekeepers deputations, taxation records *etc.*

There are also the formal commissions of the peace, and records of petty sessions. Some justices also kept their own notebooks. These records are extensive, and invaluable sources for filling out the details of ancestor's lives. Many records have been published, and are listed in both *Texts and calendars*, and in the county volumes of Raymond's *British genealogical library guides.* Some of the topics they deal with are discussed elsewhere in this dictionary.

Further Reading:

- EMMISON, F.G., & GRAY, IRVINE. *County records (Quarter sessions, petty sessions, clerk of the peace and lieutenancy).* [Rev. ed.] Helps for students of history, **62.** Historical Association, 1987. Basic introduction.
- GIBSON, JEREMY. *Quarter sessions records for family historians: a select list.* 4th ed. F.F.H.S., 1995.
- HUNT, RICHARD. 'Quarter sessions order books' in MUNBY, L.M., ed. *Short guides to records. First series. 1-24.* [Rev. ed.]. Historical Association, 1994, 113-6.
- PEYTON, S.A., ed. *Minutes of proceedings in Quarter Sessions held for the Parts of Kesteven in the County of Lincoln, 1674-1695.* 2 vols. Lincoln Record Society **25-6.** 1931. Includes extensive introduction.

- EMMISON, F.G., *Elizabethan life: disorder, mainly from Essex sessions and assize records.* Chelmsford: Essex County Council, 1970.
- FRASER, C.M., ed. *Durham Quarter Sessions rolls 1471-1625.* Surtees Society **199**. 1991.

Quitclaim

A formal renunciation of any claim to property which is not in the possession of the person making the quitclaim.

R

Rapes

Rapes are ancient administrative areas of Sussex; each includes several hundreds.

Rates

Rates could be levied by parishes for a variety of purposes, e.g. church maintainance, bridge repairs, poor relief, *etc.* Rate lists can often be found amongst *parish records, in the accounts of *churchwardens, *overseers of the poor, *etc.* They were based on an assessment of the yearly value of property and list householders and / or owners. A few boroughs also had the right to levy rates. In the twentieth century rates were a prime source of local government finance, and rate books are a useful source to compare with *electoral registersand other lists of names.

Further Reading:

- DARLINGTON, IDA. 'Rate books', in MUNBY, L.M., ed. *Short guide to records first series, guides 1-24.* [Rev.ed.] Historical Association, 1994, 21-4.

Reconstitution

See Family Reconstitution

Record Offices

Record offices house the archives that family historians depend upon. *County record offices are likely to be of most use to researchers, since they hold documents such as parish registers and wills. The *Public Record Office holds many of the documents mentioned in this dictionary. The *British Library's Manuscripts Dept., and its *Oriental and India Office Collections also hold very substantial archival materials, as do many universities, museums, learned societies, businesses and other institutions (some of which are mentioned in this dictionary).

The function of the record office is to collect and preserve *archives, and to make them available by listing, indexing, and calendaring them. In view of their unique nature, preservation is regarded as more important than production. Users are expected to treat original documents with respect, not to mark or damage them in any way, and always to use pencil, rather than pen, when taking notes.

Web Pages:

* You and your Record Office: a code of practice for family historians using record offices
  www.ffhs.org.uk/General/Help/Record.htm

* Archon
  www.hmc.gov.uk/archon/archon.htm
  Authoritative listing of record office web-sites

* English Record Offices and Archives on the Web
  www.oz.net/~markhow/englishros.htm

Further Reading:

* GIBSON, J., & PESKETT, H. *Record Offices: how to find them.* 9th ed. F.F.H.S., 2002. Includes maps.
* COLE, JEAN, & CHURCH, ROSEMARY. *In and around record repositories in Great Britain and Ireland.* 4th ed. ABM Publishing, 1998. Detailed list of repositories.

Record Societies

Record societies exist in order to publish texts, calendars, indexes, *etc.,* of documents of interest to their members. A large number of societies exist; most focus on particular counties, but others cover subjects as diverse as *Catholic records, *heraldic visitations, and *pipe rolls. The county volumes of Raymond's *British genealogical library guides,* list relevant volumes. A full listing of record society publications is given in * *Texts and calendars.*

Recovery Rolls

See Common Recovery

Recto

The right hand side of an open book, the opposite of *verso*. Manuscript volumes are often numbered using the superscript 'r' or 'v'.

Rectors and Vicars

The rector was the priest presented to the bishop by the patron for institution to a parochial benefice. He was entitled to occupy the glebe, and to the tithes of the parishioners. Responsibilities included the conduct of church services, the spiritual welfare of parishioners, and maintainance of the chancel. Many parishes were appropriated to monasteries and other ecclesiastical institutions, who kept the 'great tithes', giving 'small tithes' to a vicar who served as priest in their place. After the dissolution, rectorial tithes which had been monastic property were often purchased by lay people.

Recusant Rolls

Recusants were those who refused to attend services at their parish church. The penalty for this refusal was a fine of 1/- per absence from 1559, increased to £20 in 1581, and subsequently to the forfeiture of all goods owned and of two-thirds of real property. The recusant rolls in the *Public Record Office (E376 and E377) are annual returns, 1592-1691. Some of them have been published by the *Catholic Record Society, although it should be remembered that recusants included both Roman Catholics and protestant dissenters. Details of these publications are given in *Texts and calendars*. See also *Roman Catholics.

Further Reading:

- WILLIAMS, J. ANTHONY. 'Recusant rolls', in MUNBY, L.M., ed. *Short guides to records.* First series, 1-24. Historical Association, 1994, 63-6.

- BOWLER, HUGH, ed. *Recusant roll no.2 (1593-1594)*. Catholic Record Society **57**. 1965.

Registrar General

The officer who oversees the *civil registration of births, marriages and deaths, and who also conducts the decennial *census.

Registration District

Registration districts were originally based on *poor law union boundaries, but have undergone various changes. They are used for purposes of *civil registration, and also for the *census.

Web Pages:

- English and Welsh Register Offices
  www.genuki.org.uk/big/eng/RegOffice/

- Registration Districts in England and Wales (1837-1930)
  www.fhsc.org.uk/genuki/reg/

Further Reading:

- LANGSTONE, BRETT. *A handbook to the civil registration districts of England and Wales*. Langstone, 2001.

Regnal Years

See Dates

Relationships

We all understand the relationships of mother, father, brother, sister, uncle and aunt. Cousinage is more complicated. First cousins are the children of two siblings. Second cousins are the grand-children of two siblings. Your first cousin 'once removed' is the child of your first cousin, or your parent's first cousin; if he is 'twice removed' he / she will be the grandchild of your first cousin, or the child of your parent's first cousin.

Removals

See Settlement

Rentals

Rentals are frequently found in collections of *estate records. They are schedules listing the names of tenants, the property they occupy, and the rents due or paid. If a series of rentals is found, they will record the succession of tenants, and may consequently identify several generations of the same family. Many rentals have been published; they are listed in *Texts and calendars*, and in the county volumes of Raymond's *British genealogical library guides*.

Requests, Court of

See Court of Requests

Residence, Certificates of

See Certificates of Residence

Return of Owners of Land 1873

This survey was compiled by the government and published in the *Parliamentary papers*. It aimed to list everyone who owned more than one acre of land, and was based on information provided by rate books. County returns have been re-printed by a variety of different organisations; details are given in the county volumes of Raymond's *British genealogical library guides*.

Further Reading:

- *Owners of land, 1872-3 (England and Wales)*. 2 vols. House of Commons Parliamentary papers 1874, 72 pts 1 & 2. (C1097). H.M.S.O., 1874.

Riding

A Viking word meaning a third part. Prior to 1974, Yorkshire was divided into three ridings; the Parts of Lindsey, in Lincolnshire, was similarly divided into ridings.

Rolls

Rolls provided medieval and later administrators with one of their primary means of record keeping. They are documents written on parchment stitched together at top and bottom, and rolled up. Alternatively they may have been stitched together at the top of the membrane only, and then rolled up. The records of manorial courts are typically written on *court rolls, and some of the great national series of records which continued from medieval times to the nineteenth century were written on rolls, e.g. the *pipe rolls.

Rolls of Honour

Rolls of honour record those who died in war - usually the two world wars. Many of these were compiled by schools, employers, local councils, *etc.*, as well as by the government. Those that were published are listed in the county volumes of Raymond's *British genealogical library guides.* Both published and unpublished rolls for the First World War are listed in:

• HOLDING, NORMAN. *The location of British Army records 1914-1918.* 4th ed. F.F.H.S., 1999.

Roman Catholics

Roman Catholicism ceased to be the established religion of England in the mid-sixteenth century; those who clung to the old religion were, from 1558, officially seen as a threat to the safety of the realm, and were fined for non-attendance at church. The *recusant rolls record the fines. *Quarter sessions records also include many lists of recusants, as do a variety of other state papers. Many fled abroad and established colleges at places such as Douia, Rome, St. Omers, *etc.* The *Catholic Record Society has published a number of the registers of such colleges. They were intended to train missionary priests for the re-conversion of England. Many overseas convents were also established.

The Jacobite rebellions of 1715 and 1745 ensured that the fear of popery remained until the end of the eighteenth century. Relief Acts of 1778, 1791 and 1829 permitted the holding of services and removed legal disabilities from

Roman Catholics (*continued*)

Roman Catholics. It was not, however, until the 1840s, that numbers began to swell, with the conversion of large numbers of upper-class Anglicans, the work of Italian missionaries amongst artisans in the Midlands and South Wales, and the influx of Irish labourers in the famine years.

Roman Catholic registers were rarely kept prior to 1700; such records would have been damning evidence. However, such records did begin to be kept in the eighteenth century. Only a few were surrendered to the Registrar General in 1840 and 1857, when many nonconformist registers were handed over; however, many are now in county record offices; locations are given by Gandy's *Catholic missions...* The Roman Catholics kept records of confirmations with their registers (see *baptism). Various other lists of congregations are also available.

Web Pages:
- Catholic Recusants
  www.pro.gov.uk/leaflets/ri2173.htm
- Catholic Record Society
  www.catholic-history.org.uk/downsrev/index.htm

Further Reading:
- GANDY, MICHAEL. *Tracing your Catholic ancestors in England.* Basic facts about ... series. F.F.H.S., 1998.
- WILLIAMS, J.A. *Recusant history: sources for recusant history (1559 to 1791) in English official archives.* Catholic Record Society, 1983. Also published in *Recusant history* **16**(4), 1983, 331-470.
- SHORNEY, DAVID. *Protestant nonconformity and Roman catholicism: a guide to sources in the Public Record Office.* P.R.O. readers guide **13**. P.R.O. Publications, 1996.
- GANDY, M. *Catholic missions and registers.* 6 vols. + atlas vol. Michael Gandy, 1993.
- GANDY, M. *Catholic family history: a bibliography of general sources.* Michael Gandy, 1996.

- GANDY, M. *Catholic family history: a bibliography of local sources.* Michael Gandy, 1996.
- STEEL, D.J., & SAMUEL, EDGAR. *Sources for Roman Catholic and Jewish genealogy and family history.* National index of parish registers 3. Phillimore, for the Society of Genealogists, 1974.

Rose's Act
See Parish Registers

Royal Air Force
The Royal Air Force was founded by a merger of the Royal Flying Corps and the Royal Navy Air Service in 1918. Some of its records are in the *Public Record Office, but many are still held by the Royal Air Force. Officers are listed in the *Air Force list,* first published in 1918. Their service records for 1914-20 are available on microfilm at the Public Record Office, class AIR76.

Web Pages:
- R.A.F., R.F.C., & R.N.A.S: First World War 1914-1918 service records.
  catalogue.pro.gov.uk/Leaflets/ri2049.htm
- Royal Air Force: Second World War 1939-1945 Service Records
  catalogue.pro.gov.uk/Leaflets/ri2050.htm

Further Reading:
- SPENCER, WILLIAM. *Air Force records for family historians.* Public Record Office readers guide 21. 2000.
- WILSON, EUNICE. *The records of the Royal Air Force: how to find the few.* F.F.H.S., 1991.

Royal Commission on Historical Manuscripts
See Historical Manuscripts Commission

Royal Greenwich Hospital
The Royal Greenwich Hospital was founded in 1694 as a home for pensioned seamen and marines; the first pensioners

Royal Greewich Hospital (*continued*)

were admitted in 1705. There was also a school. Records of baptisms, marriages and burials are available in the *Public Record Office, (RG4/1669 and RG8/1669-79), as are records of admissions (ADM73), and various other archives. Greenwich pensioners did not necessarily reside at the Hospital; there were many out-pensioners.

Web Page:
- Royal Navy: Pension Records: Ratings
  www.catalogue.pro.gov.uk/leaflets/ri2294.htm

Royal Marines

The Royal Marines are soldiers recruited to fight at sea. They were first raised at the end of the seventeenth century, and have been in continuous existence since 1755.

The *Public Record Office holds a wide range of records - commissions, pay lists, service records, muster books, *etc.* It may also be possible to trace officers through the *Navy list* and the *Army list,* which are held in major reference libraries.

Web Page:
- Royal Marines: Officers Service Records
  www.catalogue.pro.gov.uk/leaflets/ri2047.htm

- Royal Marines: Other Ranks Service Records
  www.catalogue.pro.gov.uk/leaflets/ri2045.htm

- Royal Marines: How to Find a Division
  www.catalogue.pro.gov.uk/leaflets/ri2046.htm

- Royal Marines: Further Areas of Research
  www.catalogue.pro.gov.uk/leaflets/ri2048.htm

Further Reading:
- THOMAS, GARTH. *Records of the Royal Marines.* Public Record Office readers guide 10. 1995.

Royal Navy

The origins of the Royal Navy are lost in the mists of antiquity. However, Samuel Pepys reorganized naval administration in the 1660's, and from that date records began to be kept.

A wide range of archival sources are held by the *Public Record Office. Full pay and half pay registers, 1668-1920 provide brief information; passing certificates 1660-1902 record officers success in examinations and sometimes include details of service to date and baptismal certificates; the naval surveys of 1816-61 consist of letters from officers themselves giving details of service. Full service registers began to be kept in the 1840s; a variety of pension records are available.

The outline of a commissioned officer's career can be traced through published *Navy lists* which commence in 1782. A wide variety of other published sources are also available; details are given in Raymond's *Occupational sources for genealogists.* These publications are widely available in libraries.

Web Pages:

• A-Z Index of Leaflets
  www.pro.gov.uk/leaflets/Riindex.asp
  Includes a wide range of leaflets on naval records, too many to list individually here.

Further Reading:

• PAPPALARDO, B. *Tracing your naval ancestors.* Public Record Office, 2002.
• RODGER, N.A.M. *Naval records for genealogists.* Public Record Office handbooks **22**. 1988.
• *Using navy records.* Pocket guides to family history. Public Record Office, 2000.

Royalist Composition Papers

As the loosing side in the English Civil War, the royalists had their estates sequestrated, and had to compound for their recovery. The records of the two Parliamentary committees which dealt with these matters contain much useful information on royalist estates. They are in the *Public Record Office, class SP23.

Web Page:

- Crown, Church and Royalist Lands, 1642-1660
  www.pro.gov.uk/leaflets/ri2175.htm

Further Reading:

- GREEN, MARY ANNE EVERETT, ed. *Calendar of the Proceedings of the Committee for Compounding, &c., 1643-1660.* 5 vols. H.M.S.O., 1889-92.

S

St. Catherine's House
This used to house the records of *civil registration, which are now at the *Family Records Centre.

Saints Days
See Dates

Salvation Army
The Salvation Army was founded by William Booth in the late nineteenth century. It maintains registers of 'soldiers' at local corps headquarters; records of 'officers', i.e., full-time workers, are kept at the Army's Territorial Headquarters. It may not be possible to see these records, but information from them may be available. Many records are now held in the Army's International Heritage Centre, 117-21, Judd Street, King's Cross, London WC1H 9NN.

Web Page:
- The Salvation Army International Heritage Centre
  www1.salvationarmy.org/heritage.nsf

Further Reading:
- WIGGINS, RAY. *My ancestors were in the Salvation Army. How can I find out more about them?* 2nd ed. Society of Genealogists, 1999.

School Records
In the course of the last few centuries, most British children have attended school. Their attendance was usually recorded, and it is probable that many of our ancestors' names could be found amongst school records. School

School Records (*continued*)

admission registers and log books are particularly useful sources, and many of them can be found in *county record offices. Many public schools have published their admissions registers. Numerous school histories have also been published; although less likely to provide names, they do help fill in the background. Census returns record the names of pupils at boarding school. A wide variety of other records are described by Chapman.

Further Reading:

* CHAPMAN, COLIN R. *The growth of British education and its records.* 2nd ed. Dursley: Lochin Publishing, 1992.
* HORN, PAMELA. 'School log books', in THOMPSON, K.M., ed. *Short guides to records. Second series, 25-48.* Historical Association, 1997, pp.104-8.
* JACOBS, P.M. *Registers of the universities, colleges and schools of Great Britain and Ireland: a list.* Athlone Press, 1966.
* *School, university and college registers and histories in the library of the Society of Genealogists.* 2nd ed. Society of Genealogists, 1996.

Scotland

Scotland is a country in its own right, with quite different systems of law and land tenure; the established religion is Presbyterianism, and Gaelic is still spoken in the Highlands. There has been a great deal of contact between Scotland and England; both countries had Norman kings, there have been many Anglo-Scottish wars; in 1603 James VI of Scotland became James I of England. His court attracted many Scottish courtiers to England. Many other Scottish migrants have followed where they led, and consequently many English family historians can trace Scottish connections.

Most Scottish genealogical records are housed in two institutions. The Registrar General for Scotland, New Register House, Edinburgh EH1 3YT has the general register of births, marriages and deaths from 1855. Indexes are on computer, and certificates viewable on microfiche. He also has census returns, similar to those of England, and the old parochial registers of the Presbyterian church. The National Archives of Scotland, H.M. General Register House, Edinburgh, EH1 3YY has extensive records of land-holding: services of heirs, register of sasines, registers of deeds, *etc.* It also holds probate records, assessments to hearth, poll, window and land taxes, records of the Scottish courts, and a multitude of other sources.

Web Pages:

* Genuki Scotland
  www.genuki.org.uk/big/sct

* Scots Origins: General Register Office for Scotland
  www.origins.net/GRO/

* National Archives of Scotland
  www.nas.gov.uk

Over 1,000 web pages are listed in:
* RAYMOND, STUART A. *Scottish family history on the web.* F.F.H.S., 2001.

Further Reading:

* CORY, K.B. *Tracing your Scottish ancestry.* 2nd ed. Edinburgh: Polygon, 1996.
* HAMILTON-EDWARDS, G. *In search of Scottish ancestry.* 2nd ed. Phillimore, 1983.
* MOODY, D. *Scottish family history.* B.T.Batsford, 1988.
* SINCLAIR, CECIL. *Tracing your Scottish ancestors: a guide to ancestry research in the Scottish Record Office.* Rev. ed. Edinburgh: Stationery Office, 1997.
* STEEL, D.J., & STEEL, A.E.F. *Sources for Scottish genealogy and family history.* National index of parish registers, **12.** Phillimore, 1970.
* FERGUSON, J.P.S. *Scottish family histories held in Scottish libraries.* Edinburgh: Scottish Central Library, 1960.

Scotland (*continued*)
- STEVENSON, DAVID, & STEVENSON, WENDY B. *Scottish texts and calendars: an analytical guide to serial publications.* Royal Historical Society guides and handbooks **14**. 1987.

Secretary Hand
The script commonly used in sixteenth and seventeenth-century hand-writing.

Settlement
See Poor Law

Sheriffs
The sheriff was the Crown's chief officer in each county (and also in some boroughs) in medieval times. His pre-eminence passed to the *Lord Lieutenant in Tudor times, and other duties passed to the *Justices of the Peace, *coroners, tax collectors, *etc.* However, he continued to preside at *Quarter sessions. The office is now entirely ceremonial.

Sinister
The left-hand side of a *coat of arms, viewed from the back.

Sir
This is the title of honour placed before the christian names of knights and baronets. It was also used in the medieval period before the names of priests who were not graduates (the latter were masters).

Society of Friends
The Friends, or Quakers as they are more popularly known, were founded after the upheavals of civil war in the mid-seventeenth century. Friends sought the 'inner light', and rejected formal religion, including clergy and church services. They were frequently prosecuted in *church courts and *quarter sessions, until the Act of Toleration, 1689 granted liberty of worship. In the eighteenth and nineteenth centuries, many were prominent in industry and commerce.

It is important to understand the structure of Society organization in order to undertake research. Each local society is a Particular Meeting, managed by its own Preparative Meeting. The latter sends delegates to its district's Monthly meetings (in whom all property is vested). The Monthly Meetings send delegates to the Quarterly Meeting, whose jurisdiction covers at least one county, and who, in their turn, send delegates to the spring London Yearly Meeting. This structure made possible the enforcement of strict discipline, which is reflected in the Society's records. The Society cared for its own, and its records contain much information about topics such as apprenticeship, education, care of the poor, and, of most relevance to genealogists, marriage. Permission to marry had to be sought from the Monthly Meeting, which carried out extensive enquiries before granting 'liberations'. Marrying non-quakers was strongly discouraged. Marriages usually took place by simple declaration in the regular mid-week meeting for worship.

The Friends had their own system for registering births (not baptisms - they did not practice baptism), marriages and deaths. The clerk of each Monthly Meeting registered each event that was reported to him. Pre-1837 Quaker registers were surrendered to the Registrar General in 1840, and are now in the *Public Record Office, classes RG6 and RG8. Before surrender, however, ' digests', or indexes of the registers were prepared; one set was lodged with the Quarterly Meetings (some of which are now in county record offices); another complete set for the whole country is held at Friends House, 173-7, Euston Road, London NW1 2BJ. A microfilm copy is available in some reference libraries. Friends House also holds the minutes of many Meetings, 'suffering books', admission lists, and a wide variety of other records. Some records have also been deposited in county record offices. The Society's record keeping activities mean that Friends are particularly well documented.

Web Page:

- Library Guide 2: Genealogical Sources
  www.quaker.org.uk/library/guides/libgenea.html
  Guide from Friends House Library

- Quaker Family History Society
  www.qfhs.co.uk

Further Reading:

- MILLIGAN, EDWARD H., & THOMAS, MALCOLM J. *My ancestors were Quakers: how can I find out more about them?* 2nd ed. Society of Genealogists, 1999.
- 'The Society of Friends (Quakers)'. in STEEL, D.J. *Sources for nonconformist genealogy and family history.* National index of parish registers **2**. Society of Genealogists, 1973.
- *Friends House Library digest registers of births, marriages and burials for England and Wales, 17th c. - 1837.* 32 microfilm reels. World Microfilm Publications, 1989.
- *General Register Office: Society of Friends registers, notes and certificates of births, marriages and death, (RG6).* List & Index Society **267**. 1996.
- MORTIMER, JEAN, & MORTIMER, RUSSELL, eds. *Leeds Friends minute book 1692 to 1712.* Yorkshire Archaeological Society record series **139**. 1980.
- RACE, HAROLD W., ed. *The first minute book of the Gainsborough Monthly Meeting of the Society of Friends 1669-1719.* 3 vols. Lincoln Record Society **38, 40,** & **42.** 1948-51.

Society of Genealogists

The Society of Genealogists is the major family history society in the U.K. It publishes the *Genealogists magazine,* runs an extensive range of lectures and courses, is one of the leading genealogical publishers, and maintains one of the most important libraries devoted to family history in the country. Its address is: Charterhouse Buildings, Goswell Road, London EC1M 7BA

- The Society of Genealogists
  www.sog.org.uk

Solemn League and Covenant

This was an oath of allegiance required by Parliament in 1644 of all males aged over 18. At the time the country was divided by war, so the oath could only be enforced in areas under Parliamentary control. Returns were kept with parish records; those few which are known are listed by Gibson and Dell.

Further Reading:
- GIBSON, JEREMY, & DELL, ALAN. *The Protestation returns 1641-1642 and other contemporary listings.* F.F.H.S., 1995.

Somerset House

The former home of the Principal Probate Registry (see *probate records).

Son in Law

This term frequently had the meaning, 'step-son'.

South Africa

The earliest European settlers at the Cape of Good Hope were the Dutch, who opened a victualling station on the route to the East Indies in 1652. It was not until 1795 that the British occupied the Cape in order to keep the French out, and not until 1806 that their occupation became permanent. 4,800 early pioneers are listed by Philip.

A further 4,500 British assisted emigrants arrived in 1820; in 1849-51 4,000 arrived in Natal. Many more followed when gold was discovered in the Cape Province in 1866, and in the Transvaal in the mid 1880's. After the Boer Wars many British soldiers decided to remain.

A few records are in the *Public Record Office - mainly Colonial Office correspondence and service records *etc.* for

South Africa (*continued*)

Boer War soldiers (see *Army). Most relevant records of English emigration are likely to be found in South African repositories.

Web Pages:

- South African Genealogy
  home.global.co.za/~mercon/

Further Reading:

- LOMBARD, R.T. *Handbook for genealogical research in South Africa.* 3rd ed. Pretoria: H.S.R.C., 1990.
- PHILIP, P. *British residents at the Cape 1795-1819: biographical record of 4,800 pioneers.* Cape Town: David Philip, 1981.
- HOCKLEY, H.E. *The story of the British settlers of 1820 in South Africa.* 2nd ed. Cape Town: Juta & Co., 1957. Includes list.
- BULL, E. *Aided immigration from Britain to South Africa, 1857 to 1867,* ed. J.L.Basson. Pretoria: Human Sciences Research Council, 1991.
- SPENCER, S.O. *British settlers in Natal 1824-1857: a biographical register.* 6 vols. to date. Pietermaritzburg: University of Natal Press, 1981- .

Spelling

Samuel Johnson and Nathan Bailey, the first dictionary makers, have a great deal to answer for! They were largely responsible for popularising the notion that there is such a thing as 'correct' spelling. Before their day, spelling was not standardised. It is particularly important that family historians appreciate this fact, since surnames were liable to be spelt in a variety of different ways. The clerks who wrote our ancestors' names frequently had only the sound of the spoken word to go on, hence Raymond, Raymund, Reymond, Raymont were all possible spellings of the same name. Consequently, when searching records for particular surnames, it is vital that all variants of the name be noted.

Star Chamber
   See Court of Star Chamber

State Papers Domestic
   The state papers domestic cover an extraordinarily diverse range of subjects; they are the papers of the Secretary of State, and, in amongst the policy papers and proclamations, ecclesiastical, military and economic affairs, there is much biographical information. They have mostly been fully calendared; some have also been microfilmed.

Web Page:
- State Papers Domestic: Edward VI - Charles I, 1547-1649
  www.catalogue.pro.gov.uk/leaflets/ri2123.htm
  A number of further leaflets cover the period to 1782.

Further Reading:
- *Calendar of state papers, domestic series of the reigns of Edward VI, Mary, Elizabeth, [James I] ...* 12 vols. H.M.S.O., 1856-77. Many further volumes cover the period to 1704.
- *The complete state papers domestic.* Many microfilm reels. Harvester Press, 1977. Microfilm of the original documents, 1547-1702.
- *Unpublished state papers of the English Civil War and Interregnum.* 114 microfilm reels. Harvester Press, 1975-8.

Strays
   A 'stray', to the genealogist, is a record of an individual found in an area where he was not born. Usually, but not always, this is interpreted as 'out of county'. The Federation of Family History Societies' strays clearing house collects records of strays in birth, marriage and death registers, in the census, *etc.*, and has thus far issued 4 collections on microfiche. Many *family history societies have also issued collections of strays, and some of their journals regularly publish lists.

- The Strays Clearing House and the National Strays Index
  www.ffhs.org.uk/General/Help/Strays.htm

Subsidy
See Lay Subsidy

Supporters
In heraldry, where the shield is depicted as supported by beasts, real or mythical, these are designated supporters. The right to supporters is limited to peers, knights of the garter, and a handful of other categories.

Supreme Court of Judicature
The Supreme Court was found in 1875 by amalgamating the superior courts of civil and common law, and fusing their jurisdiction: it consists of the High Court of Justice and the Court of Appeal. The High Court was divided into Queen's Bench, Common Pleas, Exchequer, Chancery, and Probate Divorce & Admiralty Divisions; in 1881, Common Pleas and Exchequer were amalgamated with Queen's Bench. Further changes took place in 1971.

Records of cases heard in the Court of Appeal are held in the Public Record Office, (J83-84), but give minimal information. Records of the High Court are filed by type rather than case; they are also in the Public Record Office, but it can be time consuming to identify all the documentation relating to a particular case. Minimal information is available after 1945. Records include decrees and orders, pleadings, affidavits, depositions, petitions, reports, *etc.*

Web Pages:
- Supreme Court, Chancery Division: Cases after 1875
  catalogue.pro.gov.uk/Leaflets/ri2246.htm

- Supreme Court: Appeal Cases after 1875
  catalogue.pro.gov.uk/Leaflets/ri2247.htm

Surnames

Surnames did not come into general use in England until the twelfth century, and it was not until the fifteenth century that they became universal. In Wales, adoption of fixed surnames came even later. Surnames were obviously useful to distinguish people with the same christian names - and the range of christian names used in Norman England was narrow - but that does not explain why they became hereditary. Indeed, many early 'surnames' were in fact by-names, and not hereditary; it is possible to find documentary evidence of the same person being referred to by several different by-names.

Surnames were derived from a wide range of sources: place-names, occupational terms, nick-names, paternal names, *etc.* Their origins, locations and distribution have been studied in considerable depth; such studies are of obvious relevance to the genealogist, who usually assumes that the same surname has been borne by his forefathers for at least half a millenia. It is a dangerous assumption! Surnames have been subjected to many changes over the centuries. Particular surnames may not have had a standardised *spelling, and the genealogist must keep a continual look-out for variants. Townend, for example, might be Townsend; Dunn might be Donne, Smith might be Smythe - and indexes to original sources may not bring all the variants together. *By-names may have replaced older surnames, as may *aliases. There may have been deliberate changes of surname for purposes of inheritance (amongst the *gentry especially); new surnames may have been invented for deserted children. There are a whole host of reasons why your surname may be different from that of your ancestors, some of which are discussed at length by Redmonds.

Further Reading:

- McKINLEY, RICHARD. *A history of British Surnames.* Longman, 1990.

Surnames (*continued*)

- REANEY, P.H. *The origin of English surnames.* Routledge & Kegan Paul, 1967.
- REDMONDS, GEORGE. *Surnames and genealogy: a new approach.* F.F.H.S., 2002.
- TITFORD, JOHN. *Searching for surnames: a practical guide to their meanings and origins.* Newbury: Countryside Books, 2002.
- REANEY, P.H. *A dictionary of English surnames.* 3rd ed. Routledge, 1991.
- HANKS, PATRICK, & HODGES, FLAVIA. *A dictionary of surnames.* Oxford: Oxford University Press, 1988.
- REDMONDS, GEORGE. *Yorkshire West Riding.* English surnames series 1. Phillimore, 1973. Similar volumes in this series are available for several other counties.
- MORGAN, T.J., & MORGAN, PRYS. *Welsh surnames.* Cardiff: University of Wales Press, 1985.
- ROWLANDS, J., & ROWLANDS, S. *The surnames of Wales.* F.F.H.S., 1996.
- 'Surnames', in STEEL, D.J., *et al. Sources of births, marriages and deaths before 1837 (1).* National index of parish registers 1. Society of Genealogists, 1968, 88-100.

Surrender

A surrender extinguishes an owners' right in a property. The three-life lease was often surrendered in order to make a new lease, and thus extend the tenancy of the lessee.

Surveys

Estate surveys, common in the sixteenth and seventeenth centuries, provide detailed descriptions of particular estates, including the names of tenants, *entry fines and rents, *etc.,* the properties held, names of previous tenants, *etc.* They will usually be found with other *estate records, and are sometimes accompanied by *maps. Parliamentary surveys of crown lands, made during the *interregnum, with a view to their sale, are similar in character.

Further Reading:

- KERRIDGE, ERIC. ed. *Surveys of the manors of Philip, first Earl of Pembroke and Montgomery, 1631-2.* Wiltshire Archaeological and Natural History Society Records Branch, **9**. 1953. Manors in Wiltshire
- NEWTON, S.C. 'Parliamentary surveys', in MUNBY, L. M. *Short guides to records. First series 1-24.* [Rev. ed.] Historical Association, 1994, 89-92.
- POUNDS, NORMAN J.G. ed. *The Parliamentary survey of the Duchy of Cornwall.* 2 vols. Devon & Cornwall Record Society. New series **25-** & **27**. 1982-4.

T

Taxation

The records of taxation include innumerable lists of
taxpayers. Assessments for the *lay subsidy, *hearth tax,
*poll tax, and *land tax abound in the *Public Record Office;
*county record offices also hold many land tax assessments,
a few *window tax records, and a wide variety of
assessments to local *rates, *etc.* These tax lists are
invaluable sources for locating people in the past; where a
run of assessments survive they may identify different
family members, and enable the descent of property to be
traced. Jurkowski, *et al* provide a full listing of taxes levied
prior to 1688. Many tax lists have been published by record
societies; these may be identified in *Texts and calendars*,
and in the county volumes of Raymond's *British
genealogical library guides.*

Web Page:
- Taxation Records before 1660
  www.pro.gov.uk/leaflets/ri2117.htm

Further Reading:
- JURKOWSKI, M., SMITH, C.L., & CROOK, D. *Lay taxes in
  England and Wales, 1188-1688.* Public Record Office
  handbook, **31.** P.R.O.Publications, 1998.
- HOYLE, R.W. *Tudor taxation records: a guide for users.*
  Public Record Office readers guide **5.** 1994.

Telephone Directories

The earliest telephone directory dates from 1880. Their
regular publication throughout the twentieth century means
that access to a run of them will enable you to track down
most phone subscribers, and to identify when they became

subscribers and when they ceased. Their importance increases as the importance of trade directories decreases, and they almost totally replace the latter as a useful genealogical source after 1950.

The best collection of phone directories is held at British Telecom Archives; this must be viewed on microfilm by appointment. *Guildhall Library has a good collection. Many libraries and county record offices have collections of recent - and sometimes older - directories. Those held by the *Society of Genealogists are listed by Newington-Irvine.

Web Site:
- B.T. Archives
  www.groupbt.com/Corporateinformation/BTArchives/

Further Reading:
- BRETT, DONALD. 'The use of telephone directories in surname studies', *Local historian* **16**(7), 1985, 392-404.
- NEWINGTON-IRVINE, N.J.N. *Directories and poll books in the library of the Society of Genealogists.* 6th ed. Society of Genealogists, 1995.

Tenths and Fifteenths
Fractions used in the assessment of *lay subsidies.

Tenure
After the Norman Conquest, all land was deemed to be held of the King. The King granted it to his barons as tenants in chief. They in turn granted manors to their retainers to hold by knight service. Manorial lords then let their lands to tenants, for money and / or service.

By the early modern period, there were three main types of tenure: *freehold, *leasehold, and *copyhold.

Terriers
Terriers record details of the location and size of properties on a manor or estate. Sometimes they include the names of tenants. See also *glebe terriers.

Test Act 1672/3

Together with the Corporation Act of 1661, this required those accepting public or military office to take oaths of allegiance and to obtain a certificate from their local clergy or churchwardens confirming that they had received the sacrament. This excluded Roman Catholics and nonconformists from these offices. Sacrament certificates may be found in the *Public Record Office (C224, E196 and KB22), and with *Quarter Sessions records.

Texts and Calendars

Texts and calendars is the major *bibliography of *record society publications, and should be consulted in order to identify the innumerable transcripts and indexes of original sources which these societies have published. These include documents such as wills, ecclesiastical and heraldic visitation records, deeds, letters, accounts, feet of fines, *etc., etc.* The two published volumes are continued by the web page. No family historian can afford to neglect this work.

Web Page:

• Texts and calendars since 1982: a survey
  www.hmc.gov.uk/socs/list.htm

Further Reading:

• MULLINS, E.L.C. *Texts and calendars: an analytical guide to serial publications.* Royal Historical Society guides and handbooks, **7**. 1958.
• MULLINS, E.L.C. *Texts and calendars II: an analytical guide to serial publications, 1957-1982.* Royal Historical Society guides and handbooks, **12**. 1983.

Tithes

Between the eighth and the twentieth centuries, the Biblical injunction to give a tenth of one's income - a tithe - for the work of God was a legal obligation. Precisely how the tithe was assessed varied from parish to parish; details are frequently given in *glebe terriers. Originally they were payable in kind, but this was frequently commuted to a money payment. Lists of tithepayers may sometimes be found with *parish records. The Tithe Commutation Act 1836 converted tithes into rent payments based on the prevailing price of grain. It necessitated the drawing up of tithe maps and apportionments for 11,395 English and Welsh parishes and townships. Between them, these list all landowners and tenants and their fields, and effectively provide a census of householders. Duplicate records were made, and copies are likely to be held by both the *Public Record Office (IR29 & IR30) and *county record offices.

Web Pages:
- Tithe Records: a detailed examination
  catalogue.pro.gov.uk/Leaflets/ri2148.htm

- The History of Tithes
  www.telbin.demon.co.uk/westendlhs/tithehistory.html

Further Reading:
- EVANS, ERIC J., & CROSBY, ALAN G. *Tithes: maps, apportionments and the 1836 act: a guide for local historians.* 3rd ed. British Association for Local History, 1997.
- EVANS, ERIC J. *The contentious tithe: the tithe problem and English agriculture, 1750-1850.* Routledge and Kegan Paul, 1976.
- FOOT, W. *Maps for family history: a guide to the records of the tithe, Valuation Office, and national farm surveys of England and Wales, 1836-1943.* Public Record Office reader's guide **9**. 1994.
- MUNBY, LIONEL M. 'Tithe apportionments and maps', in MUNBY, L.M., ed. *Short guides to records. First series, 1-24.* Rev. ed. Historical Association, 1994, 101-4.
- *Inland Revenue: tithe maps and apportionments (I.R.29, I.R.30).* 2 vols. List and Index Society, **68** & **83**. 1971-2.
- SANDELL, R.E. ed. *Abstracts of Wiltshire tithe apportionments.* Wiltshire Record Society **30**. 1975.

Title Deeds

Title deeds convey land from one party to another. They differ from *indentures in that they are made by one party only. Deeds provide information about vendors and purchasers, and are often found with 'abstracts of title', which record previous deeds relating to the same property. They are essential documents for tracing the descent of particular properties, and often reveal family relationships.

Deeds can be found in virtually every record office, but they are widely dispersed; with the exception of the deeds registries of Yorkshire, Middlesex, and the Bedford levels, there was no central registration of *deeds until the twentieth century. It is unlikely that any *county record office will hold all the deeds for any particular place, although they are likely to hold some for every place in their area. The *Public Record Office and the *British Library both hold vast numbers of deeds, as do many other repositories. The *National Register of Archives may be able to help locate relevant deeds.

Web Page:
- Land Conveyances: Enrolment of Deeds and Registration of Title
  www.pro.gov.uk/leaflets/ri225.htm

Further Reading:
- ALCOCK, N.W. *Old title deeds: a guide for local and family historians.* 2nd ed. Chichester: Phillimore, 2001.
- DIBBEN, A.A. *Title deeds.* Rev. ed. Helps for students of history **72.** 1990.
- CARR, A.D. 'Deeds of title', in MUNBY, L.M., ed. *Short guides to records. First series, 1-24.* [Rev. ed.] Historical Association, 67-72.
- PUGH, R.B., ed. *Calendar of Antrobus deeds before 1625.* Wiltshire Archaeological and Natural History Society Records Branch **3.** 1947.

Tokens

See Trade Tokens

Toleration Act 1689

This act modified the penal laws against nonconformists (but not *Roman Catholics or *Unitarians) allowing them to establish their own 'meeting houses'. Such houses had to be licensed, and the records of this (held with diocesan records) are prime sources for nonconformist history.

Tontines

Tontines were loans made by a fixed number of investors, who received an annuity until the last survivor of the annuitants died. As each annuitant died, his share was apportioned to the survivors. Thus the last surviving annuitant would receive the interest from the whole of the original investment. The records of eighteenth-century tontines are in the Public Record Office, classes ND02 and ND03. The registers give the names and places of abode of subscribers and their nominees, together with the ages, dates of death, and executors of the latter.

Further Reading

- LEESON, F.L. *A Guide to the records of British state tontines and life annuities of the 17th and 18th centuries.* Pinhorns, 1968.

Topographical Dictionaries

See Gazetteers and Topographical Dictionaries

Townships

Large parishes, especially in the north of England, were often divided into smaller townships for administrative purposes; these townships were responsible for poor law administration, highway maintainance, *etc.,* they were also units for purposes of taxation.

Trade Directories

The earliest trade directory was published in 1677. It was not until the late eighteenth century, however, that the earliest national directories were published, and not until 1836 that Frederick Kelly purchased the copyright of the *Post Office directory*, launching the great series of *Kelly's directories.*

The scope of directories varied widely; some covered the whole country, but others were devoted to particular towns. Most however, related to particular counties. They were usually intended to be updated regularly, sometimes annually, and many were.

The content of most directories follows a common pattern. There is an entry for each parish, beginning with a brief topographical, historical and administrative description, usually giving the names of manors, details of churches, and post office information. This is followed by a listing of the principal inhabitants, usually arranged by profession, business or trade. They do not, however, list labourers, servants or other employees.

Trade directories provide the family historian with a basic starting point. It is easy to use them to check a name or address, to identify the occupiers of particular properties, to trace the locations of particular surnames, or to compare entries in them with entries in the *census. They do, however, present some problems which may not be immediately apparent. Firstly, when they were issued they were likely to be six months out of date. Secondly, their coverage is patchy, usually being less complete in smaller villages and hamlets, and fuller in major cities. Thirdly, they are biased in favour of individuals who had some social or economic clout. Those at the bottom of the social hierarchy were not included.

Most *local studies libraries have good collections of trade directories for the areas they cover. Substantial nation-wide collections are also held by the *British Library, *Guildhall

Library and the *Society of Genealogists. It is, however, unusual to find provincial libraries holding directories from other areas - although there is a good collection at Birmingham Public Libraries. Most directories are rare; often only a few copies survive. Consequently, it is unlikely to be possible to borrow them via inter-library loan. However, some have been re-printed in recent years. Many are available on microfiche or CD. Full lists of original directories are given in the volumes by Norton, and by Shaw and Tipper. The county volumes of Raymond's *British genealogical library guides* also provide full listings, including details of reprints.

Web Pages:
- Trade Directories and Telephone Books at Guildhall Library **www.cityoflondon.gov.uk/leisure_heritage/libraries_ archives_museums_galleries/assets/pdf/ pb_directories.pdf**

- Trade Directory Holdings in Northern Libraries **www.genuki.org.uk/big/eng/nd/**

Further Reading:
- MILLS, DENNIS R. *Rural community history from trade directories.* Aldenham: Local Population Studies, 2001.
- NORTON, JANE E. *Guide to the national and provincial directories of England and Wales, excluding London, published before 1856.* Royal Historical guides and handbooks **5.** 1950.
- SHAW, GARETH, & TIPPER, ALLISON. *British directories: a bibliography and guide to directories published in England and Wales (1850-1950) and Scotland (1773-1950).* 2nd ed. Mansell Publishing, 1997.
- NEWINGTON-IRVINE, N.J.N. *Directories and poll-books, including almanacs and electoral rolls in the library of the Society of Genealogists.* Library sources **5.** 6th ed. Society of Genealogists, 1995.

Trade Directories (*continued*)
- ROGERS, K.H., ed. *Early trade directories of Wiltshire.* Wiltshire Record Society **47**. 1991. Extracts from pre-1855 national directories.

Trade Tokens

In the seventeenth and eighteenth centuries shortage of coin caused many tradesmen and shopkeepers to issue their own tokens. These would have been accepted at various establishments within the neighbourhood, and usually showed the trader's name or initials, his trade, and the place in which he traded, together with the value of the token.

Details of many tokens have been published; these publications may be worth checking if your ancestors were tradesmen. They are listed in the county volumes of Raymond's *British genealogical library guides,* and in his *Occupational sources for genealogists.* 2nd ed. F.F.H.S., 1996.

Further Reading:
- WHITING, J.R.S. *Trade tokens: a social and economic history.* Newton Abbot: David & Charles, 1971.
- BOYNE, WILLIAM. *Trade tokens issued in the seventeenth century in England, Wales and Ireland, by corporations, merchants, tradesmen, etc.* Rev. ed. by George C. Williamson. 3 vols. B.A.Seaby, 1967. Originally published 1889-91.

Trades

See Occupations

Transcripts

A transcript of an original document or inscription should reproduce its exact wording, spelling, abbreviations, capitalisation and punctuation. Many transcripts of genealogical sources such as *wills, *monumental inscriptions, *parish registers, *etc.,* are available. Some are still in *manuscript; others have been published by *family history societies, *record societies, *et al.* Many have been published on the *internet. These transcripts are invaluable aids to family historians, but should nevertheless be treated cautiously. Some - perhaps most - are reasonably accurate, but others are woeful. And the fact that some older transcripts have been re-published on microfiche or CD in recent years, implies nothing about their accuracy. Details taken from transcripts should always, if at all possible, be checked against the original document from which the transcript is taken.

Transportation

See Emigration and Emigrants, and Convicts and Prisoners.

U

Uncle
    In the past, the term had a wider meaning than it does today, and could be applied to any older male relative.

Unitarians
    Many *Presbyterian and *Baptist churches became *unitarian in the eighteenth century; that is, they denied the divinity of Christ. Details of their records are given by Ruston.

Further Reading:
- RUSTON, ALAN. *My ancestors were English Presbyterians or Unitarians: how can I find out more about them?* 2nd ed. Society of Genealogists, 2001.

United Kingdom
    The United Kingdom of Great Britain and Northern Ireland includes *England, *Scotland, *Wales and Northern Ireland. It does not include the crown dependencies of the *Channel Islands and the *Isle of Man; nor does it include southern Ireland, which has been an independent country since 1921.

United States of America
    The eastern seaboard of what is now the United States was first colonised by the British in the seventeenth century. The impetus behind initial emigration was partly economic, partly religious, in character. Many early settlers were recruited by trading companies; others, like the Mayflower migrants, fled religious persecution at home. Many went as bonded servants, or as transported criminals. Subsequently, for British migrants, the economic motive came more to the fore.
    The sources for genealogical research in the United States are extensive, and cannot be adequately described in the

space available here. Researchers seeking British migrants may be able to identify them in *passenger lists, which can be found in many repositories, both in Britain and the U.S. The National Archives and Records Administration, 8601, Adelphi Road, College Park, MD., 20740-6001, U.S.A. holds many; it also holds census returns (from 1790), military records, and a wide variety of other sources. Most sources however, are local in character, and likely to be held in state and county repositories. Vital records - the American term for registers of births, marriages and deaths - are state records, although rarely of interest to those seeking British ancestors, since they frequently only begin after 1906. Records of land transactions found in county court houses are important, since land was cheap, and almost every adult male owned some in the nineteenth century and earlier. Wills are most likely to be found still held by county probate courts.

Some records of British citizens in the United States are held by the *Public Record Office. For the nineteenth and twentieth centuries, there are many British consular registers of births, marriages and deaths amongst the Foreign Office archives.

Web Sites:
- Cyndis List
  www.Cyndislist.com

- Notes for Americans on Tracing their British Ancestry
  www.sog.org.uk/leaflets/americans.htm

- Transportation to America and the West Indies 1615-1776
  www.pro.gov.uk/leaflets/ri2234.htm

- Emigrants to North America after 1776
  www.pro.gov.uk/leaflets/ri2107.htm
  Click on title

- English Origins of American Colonists
  www.ancestry.com/search/rectype/inddbs/1038.htm
  Database of 17-18th c. wills of English colonists.

United States of America (*continued*)
- N.A.R.A.: US National Archives & Records Administration
  www.archives.gov/index.html

Further Reading:
- EAKLE, A., & CERNY, J. *The source: a guide book of American genealogy,* ed. Loretto Dennis Szucs & Sandra Hargreaves Luebking. Rev. ed. Salt Lake City: Ancestry Publishing, 1996.
- DRAKE, P. *In search of family history: a starting place.* 2nd ed. Bowie: Heritage Books, 1992.
- GREENWOOD, V.D. *The researchers guide to American genealogy.* 2nd ed. Baltimore: Genealogical Publishing, 1990.
- FILBY, P.W. *American and British genealogy and heraldry: a selected list of books.* 3rd ed. Boston: New England Historic Genealogical Society, 1983.

University Registers
Many lists of alumni (i.e. students) of schools and universities are available; those for Oxford and Cambridge universities are widely available in reference libraries, and ought to be checked by every genealogist. A good collection of school and college registers is held by the Society of Genealogists.

Further Reading:
- FOSTER, J. *Alumni Oxonienses 1500-1886.* 8 vols. Parker & Co., 1887-92. Reprinted in 4 vols., Kraus Reprint, 1980.
- VENN, J., & VENN, J.A. *Alumni Cantabrigienses.* Pt. 1. (1250)-1751 (4 vols). Pt. 2. 1751-1900 (6 vols.). Cambridge University Press, 1922-54.
- *School, university and college registers and histories in the library of the Society of Genealogists.* 2nd ed. Society of Genealogists, 1996.

Use
Land conveyed to trustees for the use of named individuals created a 'use'.

V

Valuation Office Survey

The 1909 Finance Act imposed a duty on the incremental value of all land in the U.K. Consequently, all land had to be valued. The Valuation Office survey records this valuation. Its field books, now in the *Public Record Office (IR58), record the names of all land-owners and occupiers, with detailed descriptions of each property. Valuation books, giving similar information, are mostly in *county record offices. Maps showing hereditaments are in the Public Record Office (IR121-35). Unfortunately there are no surname indexes, but it should be possible to identify the land-owners and occupiers in every parish in 1909.

Web Page:
- Valuation Office Records: the Finance (1909-1910) Act
  catalogue.pro.gov.uk/Leaflets/ri2153.htm

Further Reading:
- FOOT, WILLIAM. *Maps for family history: a guide to the records of the tithe, Valuation Office and national farm surveys of England and Wales 1836-1943.* Public Record Office readers guide **9**. 1994.
- SHORT, BRIAN, & REED, MICK. *Landownership and society in Edwardian England and Wales: the Finance (1909-10) Act 1910 records.* University of Sussex, 1987.
- SHORT, BRIAN, & REED, MICK. 'An Edwardian land survey: the Finance (1909-10) Act 1910 records', *Journal of the Society of Archivists* **8**(2), 1986, 95-103.
- SHORT, BRIAN. *Land and Society in Edwardian Britain.* Cambridge University Press, 1997.

- SHORT, BRIAN. 'The Lloyd George Finance Act material' in THOMPSON, K.M., ed. *Short guides to records. Second series, 26-48.* Historical Association, 1997, 63-9.

Vehicle Registration

Do you know the registration numbers of any cars owned by members of your family? If so, you may be able to trace details of the car and its owner. Most surviving pre-1977 vehicle registration records are now in *county record offices, and are listed by Riden.

Further Reading:

- RIDEN, PHILIP. *How to trace the history of your car: a guide to motor vehicle registration records in the British Isles.* 2nd ed. Cardiff: Merton Press, 1998.
- DUCKHAM, BARON F. 'Early motor vehicle licence records and the local historian', *Local historian* **17**, 1986-7, 351-7.

Verso

See Recto

Vestry

Originally a meeting room within a church, which gave its name to the governing body of the parish. The latter included the *incumbent, the *churchwardens, and some of the more substantial parishioners, who might be co-opted by existing members, or elected, depending on parochial custom.

The vestry became the basic unit of local government in the sixteenth and seventeenth centuries. It appointed the *constable, the overseers of the poor, and the surveyors of the highways; it supervised relief of the poor, the maintainance of law and order, and the upkeep of parish property. *Justices of the Peace, acting through *Quarter Sessions, provided general oversight of its activities. In the nineteenth century, its civil responsibilities were mostly transferred to other authorities.

Vicars

See Rectors and Vicars

Vicar General
The deputy of a bishop or archbishop. His tasks were primarily administrative in character.

Victoria County History
The aim of this series is to provide a detailed history of every county and parish in England. For each county, there are a number of volumes dealing with general subjects such as political, social and economic history, archaeology, religious houses, domesday book, *etc.* These are followed by individual histories of all the towns and parishes in the county; the latter are regarded as authoritative, and are essential sources of background information for genealogists. The series is extensive, but far from completion.

Web Page:
• Victoria History of the Counties of England
  ihr.sas.ac.uk/uch/

Further Reading:
• PUGH, R.B. *The Victoria History of the counties of England: general introduction.* Oxford University Press, for the Institute of Historical Research, 1970. Supplement 1990.

View of Frankpledge
See Manors

Villein
Villeins were manorial tenants, bound to their lord, and required to undertake work for him, but having the right to a manorial holding in accordance with the custom of the *manor. They had virtually disappeared by the sixteenth century.

Visitations
See *Ecclesiastical Visitations, and *Heraldic Visitations

Vital Records

An American term for records of births, marriages and deaths.

Volunteer Forces

Volunteer forces were raised during the Napoleonic wars, and again from 1859. In 1908 they were amalgamated with the Yeomanry to form the Territorial Force, and in 1920 became the Territorial Army. For much of their existence the Volunteers were not paid from public funds; hence records are sparse, although some may be found in the *Public Record Office and *county record offices.

Further Reading:

- SPENCER, WILLIAM. *Records of the Militia and Volunteer forces from 1757.* Public Record Office readers guide **3**. 1993.

W

Wales

Wales has had the same system of government as England since Tudor times, except that the *Court of Great Sessions fulfilled the role of assize courts in Wales. However, a number of important differences should be noted by researchers. Firstly, patronymic *surnames survived as late as the nineteenth century in some parts of the principality, i.e. children took their father's forename as a surname. Secondly, an acquaintance with the Welsh language may be needed in order to read some documents. Thirdly, documentary survival in Wales has not been as good as in England; early parish registers, for example, are frequently missing. Finally, the incidence of nonconformity was greater in Wales than in England, and this is reflected in parish and nonconformist records.

The major repository is the *National Library of Wales; it holds many sources which, in England, would be in a county record office.

Web Page:
- Wales
  www.genuki.org.uk/big/wal

- Wales Gen Web
  www.walesgenweb.com/

Further Reading:
- ROWLANDS, JOHN, & ROWLANDS, SHEILA, eds. *Welsh family history: a guide to research.* 2nd ed. F.F.H.S., 1998.
- ISTANCE, JEAN, & CANN, E.E. *Researching family history in Wales.* F.F.H.S., 1996.

- WILLIAMS, C.J., & WATTS-WILLIAMS, J. *The parish registers of Wales / Cofresti Plwyf Cymru.* 2nd ed. National Library of Wales, 2000.

Wapentake

The equivalent of the Hundred in the Danelaw, i.e. Derbyshire, Leicestershire, Lincolnshire, Nottinghamshire, and parts of Yorkshire.

War Graves

See Commonwealth War Graves Commission

War Memorials

War Memorials list the names of those who fell in war, and may be seen not only in prominent public places, but also in schools, hospitals, places of business, *etc., etc.* A national inventory is currently in progress. Many have been copied or photographed for the internet; Raymond provides a detailed listing of web pages.

Web Page:
- U.K. National Inventory of War Memorials
  www.iwm.org.uk/collections/niwm/

Further Reading:
- RAYMOND, STUART A. *War memorials on the web.* 2 vols. F.F.H.S., 2003.

War Office Records

The extensive records of the War Office date from 1660 onwards, and are in the Public Record Office. They provide the primary source of information for tracing ancestors who served in the Army.

Further Reading:
- ROPER, MICHAEL. *The records of the War Office and related departments, 1660-1964.* Public Record Office handbooks **29**. 1998.

Wardship

See Court of Wards and Liveries

Web Page Design

Many individual genealogists are now creating their own web pages, with the consequence that the amount of genealogical information on the internet is rapidly expanding. The technical aspects of web page design are outside the scope of this book; however, it would help fellow researchers if (a) your URL could be kept as brief, memorable and informative as possible, and (b) you give each page an informative title, i.e. not just 'genealogy' or 'parish register information', but including family and / or place-names, *etc.* It is not of any help to create a web-page without indicating the source of the data or the place it relates to. Yet many such sites exist! You should also remember to give your e-mail address, and avoid, as far as possible, changing your URL.

Further Reading:

• CHRISTIAN, PETER. *Web publishing for genealogy.* 2nd ed. David Hawgood, 1999.

Williams Library, Dr.

See Dr. Williams Library

Wills

Large numbers of pre-nineteenth century wills survive in English archives. However, not everyone made a will. Wives, for example, rarely did; their wills required their husbands' consent. Those who made wills, for the most part, had widows, younger sons, or minors to provide for, and they had something worth leaving. The majority of will-makers were men of some substance, although wills of some poor men do survive. Will-makers also had time to make their wills before they died.

Wills (*continued*)

Most wills were written when it became apparent that death was imminent. Usually, they begin with the invocation of the deity and small legacies to the church or the poor; the main body of the will consists of legacies to family and friends; the executor (who is also usually the residuary legatee) is named, and those present at the will-making add their signatures as witnesses.

It was usual for all living children to be named in a will. The fact that some only received a minimal legacy probably means that the testator had already established them on a farm or in some occupation. Widows were named too. Wealthier testators sometimes named other legatees - servants, friends, patrons, more distant relations, *etc.* Children who had died, however, were unlikely to be named.

Wills are only concerned with the moveable goods and chattels of the deceased. Consequently, they do not mention real property, other than *leasehold property (leases were treated as chattels). They may therefore, give a mis-leading picture of testators' legacies.

Executors were usually those who stood to benefit most from the will. Widows were often named as executrixes, especially when children were minors. So were younger sons. The eldest son was rarely an executor: he inherited his father's landed property, and so did not usually receive a substantial legacy in his father's will.

The process of proving wills and the courts in which they were proved are discussed under *probate records. See also *probate inventories.

Further Reading:

- *Using wills.* Pocket guides to family history. Public Record Office, 2000.
- FRANCE, R. SHARPE. 'Wills', in MUNBY, L.M., ed. *Short guides to records. First series, 1-24.* [Rev.ed.] Historical Association, 1994, 59-62.

- DARLINGTON, IDA. ed. *London Consistory Court wills 1492-1547.* London Record Society **3**. 1967.
- THWAITE, HARTLEY, ed. *Abstracts of Abbotside wills 1552-1688.* Yorkshire Archaeological Society record series, **130**. 1968.

Window Tax

The window tax was introduced in 1696 and repealed in 1851. There were a number of changes in the way it was assessed; however, it was basically a tax on inhabited houses supplemented by a tax on windows. Few returns now survive, but it may be worth checking those that do: they list taxpayers, giving the number of windows and the tax paid.

Further Reading:

- GIBSON, JEREMY, MEDLYCOTT, MERVYN, & MILLS, DENNIS. *Land and window tax assessments.* 2nd ed. F.F.H.S., 1998.

Workhouse

See Poor Law

World Wars I & II

See Army, Medals, Rolls of Honour, Royal Air Force, Royal Navy, War Memorials

Writing

The reader of this book is likely to read many more books before he / she is ready to write up the results of research. However, it is advisable to be aware of at least some of the techniques of writing a family history from the outset of research. The importance of adequate citation of references, for example, needs to be understood from the first. When you actually begin to write you will need to ask questions such as:

- who am I writing for?
- what do you expect your readers to know already?
- how can the material best be organized?
- what style is appropriate?

Writing (*continued*)

You will need a catchy title if you want to produce a book likely to sell. Be aware that you will probably have to find a printer and pay the cost of production yourself: commercial publishers are unlikely to be interested in the history of a particular family. You may, however, be able to publish articles on your research in a family history society journal, or in the transactions of a local historical society.

Further Reading:

- TITFORD, JOHN. *Writing and publishing your family history*. F.F.H.S., 1996.

Y

Yeoman

This term was applied to substantial tenant farmers between the sixteenth and the nineteenth centuries, although it had earlier been applied to the retainers of a knight, or to minor royal household servants - hence the 'yeomen of the guard'.

Yeomanry

The Yeomanry were volunteer cavalry militia, liable for home service only. These were first raised during the French revolutionary wars, and continued in operation throughout the nineteenth century. They were amalgamated with the Volunteers in 1908 to form the Territorial Force, which became the Territorial Army in 1920. Few records survive in the Public Record Office; they are more likely to be found in county record offices.

Further Reading:

- MORGAN, PAUL. *The Warwickshire Yeomanry in the nineteenth century: some fresh aspects.* Dugdale Society occasional papers **36**. 1994.